Stu has put together much powerfu ... be a more godly, and hence more ef ... I used his book for our annual executive offsite, focusing on specific chapters selected by the team members. Everyone thoroughly enjoyed the book, and we each came away with valuable insights and motivation on how to better incorporate God and His teachings in our day-to-day lives—not only as leaders and team members, but also as spouses, parents, friends and individuals.

—GUY GARDNER
PRESIDENT, WILLIAMSON FREE SCHOOL OF MECHANICAL TRADES
FORMER SPACE SHUTTLE ASTRONAUT
FORMER COMMANDER, U.S. AIR FORCE TEST PILOT SCHOOL
AND NASA AND FAA EXECUTIVE

I had the privilege to preview the manuscript of *The Grace Goes With the Chair*. I believe that this is a book everyone needs to read. Stu's years of leadership in the Air Force, commanding thousands of men and women during his career, was solidly founded on biblical leadership principles. Further, he refined these principles as a pastor and church-association executive. The book will help you no matter where you are in your leadership journey...in every area of your life.

—ARNI JACOBSON
AUTHOR, FORMER MEGA-CHURCH PASTOR
EXECUTIVE, GRACE INTERNATIONAL

Stu Johnson is one of the most gifted leaders of our day. Through his career in the Air Force leading thousands of troops and civilian employees and the last decade of overseeing thousands of pastors as the Executive Administrator of Grace International, he knows the "chair" of leadership better than anyone I know. For those who want to be effective leaders, learning from those who have mastered the journey is essential. From his many years of experience, Stu deals with a leader's personal development and how to develop tools and skills that cause people to willingly and faithfully follow. A must-read for every leader and for those aspiring to be!

—Steve Riggle
Pastor, Grace Community Church, Houston TX
President, Grace International Churches and Ministries
President, King's University

The experiential scope of Stu Johnson's managerial and spiritual grasp as a leader provides a remarkably practical manual for all of us commissioned to lead. His background in both military and church leadership (presently staffed at a mega-church that also serves a huge church network) brings so much to the table that no reader will go away disappointed. There's a fund of wisdom and resource here that will serve you for years to come.

—Jack W. Hayford
Chancellor, The King's University, Los Angeles

The Grace Goes With the Chair is not a book to be skimmed and checked off the list. If you want to become an effective leader, then this book is a must read. Each of us need to thoroughly and thoughtfully consider, act upon, and revisit on a regular basis, the concepts in this book and their applications. This is true whether you lead a few or many, volunteers or paid, in any organizational construct.

—Kathy Roberts
Brigadier General (Retired), US Air Force

This book contains simple yet profound principles. Pastor Stu's views in the area of leadership are enlightening and unique. Because of my experience, I congratulate my friend and pastor for this great work of literature, and I am certain it will be of great benefit to those who venture into leadership roles. Readers will discover a different perspective on the area of service.

—General (Retired) Romeo Orlando Vasquez Velasquez
former Commander of the Armed Forces of Honduras

THE
GRACE
GOES WITH
THE CHAIR

STU JOHNSON
WITH ROBERT MIMS

The Grace Goes With the Chair
By Stu Johnson with Robert Mims
Published by Excel
A Charisma Media Company
600 Rinehart Road
Lake Mary, Florida 32746
www.charismamedia.com

Unless otherwise noted, all Scripture quotations are from the New King James Version. Copyright © 1982 by Thomas Nelson, Inc. Used by permission. All rights reserved.

Scripture quotations marked NIV are taken from the Holy Bible, New International Version. Copyright © 1973, 1978, 1984, International Bible Society. Used by permission.

Scripture quotations marked NLT are taken from the Holy Bible, New Living Translation, copyright © 1996, 2004, 2007 by Tyndale House Foundation. Used by permission of Tyndale House Publishers, Inc., Carol Stream, Illinois 60188. All rights reserved.

Scripture quotations marked THE MESSAGE are taken from *The Message*. Copyright © 1993, 1994, 1995, 1996, 2000, 2001, 2002. Used by permission of NavPress Publishing Group.

Scripture quotations marked AMP are taken from the Amplified® Bible, Copyright © 1954, 1958, 1962, 1964, 1965, 1987 by The Lockman Foundation. Used by permission. (www.Lockman.org)

Scripture quotations marked NASB are taken from the New American Standard Bible®, Copyright © 1960, 1962, 1963, 1968, 1971, 1972, 1973, 1975, 1977, 1995 by The Lockman Foundation Used by permission. (www.Lockman.org)

Design Director: Bill Johnson
Cover design by Nathan Morgan

Visit the author's website: www.gracegoeswiththechair.com

Library of Congress Cataloging-in-Publication Data: 2012940596
International Standard Book Number: 978-1-62136-068-1
E-book International Standard Book Number: 978-1-62136-069-8

While the author has made every effort to provide accurate telephone numbers and Internet addresses at the time of publication, neither the publisher nor the author assumes any responsibility for errors or for changes that occur after publication.

13 14 15 16 — 9 8 7 6 5 4 3 2
Printed in Canada

DEDICATION

I want to dedicate this first book to my wife of forty-three years, Debbe. She is my best friend, the love of my life, and the best gift God has given me other than the death of Jesus Christ for my sins. *Debbe, thank you for your encouragement, partnership, and inspiration.*

Also, I love and thank my two children, Andy and Lisa, who were the laboratory for many of my leadership successes and failures. Not only are they my dear children, but they are also my dear friends.

ACKNOWLEDGMENTS

IT HAS BEEN more than ten years since the Lord gave me the thought on an airplane about writing a book on leadership character. I started off with a rush, writing the first five chapters in a few weeks, and then got stalled in the middle when a writer-friend told me that *another Christian leadership book* would not be attractive to publishers.

The Lord kept the book percolating in my spirit, though. After halting for a few years, I got going. I finished the first draft a couple of years ago but did not know where to go next. A good friend, Arni Jacobson, told me to contact Bob Mims (www.mimsmedia.com).

Bob had written and edited a number of books for Arni and others; he had Arni's highest recommendation. Arni was right. Bob has taken my rough draft and made it read so much more smoothly. He has been able to put himself in my shoes and express my thoughts even better. Bob, thanks for your incredible skill and effort. Thanks also for your friendship and prayers.

I also want to thank my mom, Helen, who influenced me to give my life to Jesus Christ and planted so many good seeds in my heart.

Next, I want to thank three men, Bill Hudspeth, Gary Coombs, and Dave Malkin. Bill led me to Christ in a dormitory hall at the Air Force Academy. He took the time to share some words that forever changed my life. Gary Coombs, who is now deceased, challenged me when I was timid about sharing my faith in Christ to come out of my shell of fear and live for Him. Finally, Dave Malkin, who headed Action Life in the early 1970s, led me into living in the power of God's Holy Spirit. His influence launched Debbe and me on our faith walk.

I want to also acknowledge Pastor Don Van Hoozier, who pastored High Point Baptist Church in Macon, Georgia, for over fifty years and influenced our Christian growth more than any other person. He and other pastors were the first to confirm my call to ministry in an ordination service in 1978. Our visits and calls over the years have been an incredible encouragement.

I further thank Retired Major Generals Bernie Weiss, Bob Drewes, and Tim Malishenko and Retired General Les Lyles. I served under all four of these leaders and learned by observing and interacting with them. They each had very different leadership styles, but they all impacted my leadership journey in a very positive way.

I want to also recognize General Romeo Orlando Vasquez Velasquez, who recently retired as the Commander of the Armed Forces of Honduras. I shared most of the principles in this book with him and his staff during many visits to Honduras. He also encouraged me to finish this book. Thanks, my friend!

Thanks also to Pastor Paul Adams, who introduced me to Grace International Churches and Ministries, where I now serve as Executive Administrator. Paul has been a tremendous friend and encourager to me as a military and Christian leader. Also, thanks to Pastor Steve Riggle who is the president of Grace International and is an incredibly wise and visionary leader. I have learned much from you.

Finally, I want to commend our three family dogs, CJ, Bailey, and Rocco. They have taken thousands of prayer walks with me over the last thirty-plus years. Every morning, they eagerly waited for our walks, and on these walks God sowed many leadership lessons into my life.

TABLE OF CONTENTS

INTRODUCTION

Early on in my thirty-year career as an Air Force officer, I had a revelation—an epiphany, really—that would prove to be the foundation for everything I would learn and later teach about effective leadership. That foundation was laid as I listened with spiritual ears to the Holy Spirit's still, small voice saying, "God's grace goes with the chair."

I remember that moment with crystal clarity. Preparing for a leadership position, I was carefully—and with increasing insecurity—watching the senior officer I would be replacing go through his paces with confidence and effectiveness I admired. And, thinking ahead to when I would be expected to do his job, I suddenly felt like I was drowning in a sea of expectations.

As he addressed one challenge after another, I remember thinking to myself, *I would never have thought of that. I cannot do this job. I am going to fail!*

It was then, even as my heart began to sink, that the Lord spoke to me. My predecessor seemed to do the job with so much *grace*, I thought. To me, grace meant—and still does today—having God's wisdom, strength, courage, and stamina, and the contacts to do what you need to do.

Then the Lord softly, yet firmly, filled my mind with peace and assurance. Yes, it *was* grace that was needed, and I would have it as I grew into my new position. *The grace goes with the chair.* In other words, God's favor for me—for all who truly trust Him—empowers us as we settle into our journeys. If God puts you into a position, His grace goes with the job!

While I am convinced the *grace goes with the chair* principle is a universal one, my own journey on the leadership road has been very different from most. Later in this book, I will share more about that. But for now, here's a thumbnail sketch of my beginnings.

I grew up in Montana, and soon after graduating from high school in 1965, I began life as a cadet at the US Air Force Academy.

The academy instilled discipline and focus into my life—skills that were a good framework for the military career that followed. More important, though, was that I accepted Christ as my personal Savior my first year there. I would need both the training and, most certainly, the guidance and blessings of my Savior through the rest of my academy years and then the three decades I served in the Air Force.

That I spent such a long time in the military was ironic. At first, I had not planned on making the Air Force a career. But I found that as the years passed, I was enjoying the leadership challenges—and personal, spiritual growth—that serving my country provided. I know now that those thirty years were indeed God's plan for my life, and the experiences gained on that journey prepared me uniquely for the pastoral and ministerial leadership roles that would follow.

While answering to both God and Uncle Sam, I had assignments in no less than twelve locations, each of which tested and stretched me both professionally and as a Christian. My responsibilities were varied and challenging, and I was blessed to serve under many superb commanders—men of integrity and wisdom who honed my own leadership abilities.

As I grew under these officers' tutelage and listened to the lessons and insights of that still, small voice of God along the way, I realized that it really was a *privilege* to lead others—to live and work for a purpose beyond one's self, and to guide and mentor others along the way.

I first spread my Air Force leadership wings at age twenty-five as a lieutenant in charge of a team of three. When I retired from the military many years later, I had completed my most memorable and challenging assignment yet: as the commander of nearly six thousand people, including thirty subordinate commands, spanning the western United States and responsible for billions of dollars of Department of Defense and NASA contracts.

God had blessed me and guided me through those years in the Air Force, and when I became a civilian in 1999, He led me into a new, exciting realm of service: the ministry. I first was called to be an assistant pastor at Trinity Lutheran Church in San Pedro, California. A year later, I became the senior pastor of Sonrise Christian Center in

Sun City, California, serving a wonderful and growing congregation for eight years.

While still pastoring at Sonrise, I became a district superintendent of our church association, Grace International. Then in January 2008, I assumed my current position as that global Christian fellowship's Executive Administrator, overseeing Grace International's day-to-day operations.

The stereotype of a military commander is one of an uncompromising, sometimes dictatorial "top-down" boss who has little patience for any feedback from subordinates other than a quick, *"Yes, sir!"* While there are some who fit that description, the most successful officers I've met, worked with, and tried to emulate built sterling reputations by mixing firm yet compassionate leadership with proactive team-building.

In other words, they sought, calmly and incisively considered, and were not afraid to implement ideas from those under their command. Good leaders put aside their own egos to praise the work of their subordinates; they took an interest in their lives, and both gave—and received—trust.

So, my transition from Air Force leadership to the ministry was not as difficult as you might imagine. Early on, as a newly minted officer, I had received some advice that I never forgot. An older, wiser mentor shared some great advice: God is in charge of every assignment and detail of my life. He will send me where He chooses to grow, use, and mold me. I needed to start seeing my journey in the Air Force as under God's care and direction. I was to serve with diligence, and share the love of God wherever possible.

I embraced that advice. I remembered it at times when I felt I might lose my way. I claimed it, believed it, and found that as I honored it, *God honored me with His favor!*

This is advice that can be applied to any profession God guides you into. Our Father wants to direct your paths, to help you use the gifts He has invested in you—to shine through your life in order to touch others for Him.

While I have tried to share leadership principles by example, and occasionally with individuals under my authority, I never really thought I had that much to share on a bigger stage—certainly, not in a book!

However, God dreamed something bigger for me. I had learned some important lessons, and some years ago, I learned one more: The Lord had no intention of letting me hide that wisdom like the proverbial lamp under a basket.

In October 2000, I was asked to speak about leadership at our church association's convention. I thought, *What do I have to say to these pastors that they have not already heard, in one way or another, many times?* I was mulling that over as I was on a plane flying to Houston, where the conference was being held.

As I watched the clouds slide by, I heard God's voice speak to my heart that, actually, I had a lot to say about leadership. The Lord made it clear He had been pouring into me leadership principles, lessons, and character qualities for many years—and these blessings were too precious not to share.

My mind flooded with scenes from my life that had a common theme, one of God's clear and patient direction. He had been depositing experiences, insights, and wisdom about interpersonal relationships and much more, and now it was time for those things to be invested into His broader kingdom. That would be done through messages I could share at various forums and then expand those messages in a book on leadership.

When I did speak at the convention, God confirmed that airborne vision of mine with the response I witnessed from those pastors. I truly was amazed at how eagerly they listened and embraced the Lord's leadership principles. And they were hungry for more!

Over the next several months, I began to draw on more of those spiritual and practical deposits God had made, forming them into more messages that I shared with various gatherings, both Christian and secular.

Those leadership workshops and seminars have been well-received both within the United States and outside the country. Just one example of the latter: In 2003, I traveled to Guatemala to speak to about three hundred ministers who had gathered from all over Latin America. The response was once more enthusiastic; the word-of-mouth excitement that followed in that event's wake led to the opportunity for me to share godly leadership principles many times in neighboring Honduras—not only with church leaders but with key political and military figures in that country, as well.

It was in late 2004 the Lord told me that I had a sufficient collection of messages to begin weaving them into book form. In the years since, I've worked prayerfully doing that, as time allowed with a busy schedule.

I don't consider myself a writer. But you know what? There also were times in my life when I wondered how in the world I could be an Air Force officer, or a commander of thousands of men and women, or a pastor!

God's grace (thank God!) *goes with the chair.* And so, here it is—a book that is, first and foremost, His. If there are any imperfections in the message, they are mine. However, I am satisfied that His grace will help readers learn about and develop the inspired attitudes and character qualities that every leader needs.

It is my deepest prayer that as you read this book, whatever your challenges or profession, wherever you are on your road to becoming a godly leader, whether in the secular workplace or a church ministry, that you will see your potential as God does: *limited only by your faith.*

Chapter One

THE CHARACTER OF THE LEADER

O N THAT LIFE-CHANGING flight to the Grace International convention in Houston more than a decade ago (which I briefly mentioned in this book's introduction), the Lord impressed me to write out the letters of the word *LEADER* vertically on a piece of paper. As I prayerfully considered each of those letters, God reminded me of a corresponding character quality to go with them.

In the years since that conference, I have found the Holy Spirit likes to work through my fondness for such acrostics (using particular letters in a phrase to spell out an easy-to-remember catchword) to share the lessons of leadership He has taught me.

In the case of my message in Houston, the acrostic was *LEADER*, and by the time I had landed, I had the outline for a message discussing six key leadership qualities. Today, as then, those qualities are a great place to begin preparing hearts and minds to receive the critical grace needed to be effective, integrity-driven, godly leaders.

"L" STANDS FOR "LIVE FOR JESUS FIRST"

Consider what Jesus Himself said about this all-important trait:

> "So don't worry at all about having enough food and clothing. Why be like the heathen? For they take pride in all these things and are deeply concerned about them. But your heavenly Father already knows perfectly well that you need them, and he will give them to you if you give him first place in your life and live as he wants you to."
> —MATTHEW 6:31–33, TLB

Jesus gets right to the heart of the human condition as it applies to the struggle for faith. If we truly trust in Him, we will not worry about

1

whether God will provide our needs as we serve His kingdom. *Live for Me,* Jesus says, *and I will not forsake you.* Focus on your true purpose as a leader and a child of God.

Live for Jesus first. Of the six character qualities discussed in this chapter, I believe this is the most important. At its core, living for Christ means it is Jesus who is in charge, not us. He is the Lord—of our time, plans, desires, finances, and relationships, and of our past, present, and future.

Living for Jesus means that we seek to please and honor Him in all we say and do. Further, we recognize that we cannot do anything on our own that will eternally impact people's lives. Our prayer should be: "Jesus, just use me. Influence others through me. I don't want the credit. Help me to walk and live in the fear of the Lord, remembering that I serve the King of the universe, My Savior, the Lord Jesus Christ!"

The fear of the Lord? I know, a lot of people read or hear that phrase and bristle. We think of the word in present terms, of being terrified of something evil or threatening. God is a loving God—so loving that He took human form through His only begotten Son, Jesus, and died a horrible death on our behalf.

So, what's all this about fearing the Lord?

In the Old Testament, *yir'ah* is the Hebrew word translated into English as *fear.* The Hebrew word, however, has nuances and deeper meaning that go far beyond the fear concepts of terror or dread; fear, as we know it, is usually a gut reaction to darker, malevolent threats.

Yir'ah, when used in conjunction with the name of God, carries more of the feeling of awe, along with respect and reverence so intense that you would tremble in the presence of such holiness.

The word *fear* has similar shortcomings when translated from the Greek term used in the New Testament, *phobos.* Again, the context is more of an attitude toward the Creator—His unfathomable greatness and perfection—and the astounding realization that, insignificant by comparison as we frail human beings are, we are in awe of His placing eternal value on us and of His infinite love within us.

So, now that you understand more about what godly fear really is, let me share a Bible verse that convinced me years ago to begin praying that I would learn to walk and live in the fear of the Lord:

"Then they will call on me, but I will not answer; they will seek me diligently, but they will not find me. Because they hated knowledge and did not choose the fear of the LORD."

—PROVERBS 1:28–29

Many Christians have chosen to forget this holy fear of God in favor of seeing Christ as their spiritual "big brother" and God as their heavenly "daddy." Both those descriptions have elements of truth to them, but we forget that Jesus will one day judge the earth and that God's love goes hand in hand with God's righteousness and ultimate justice.

As the verse says, though, we need to choose the fear of the Lord to be in proper relationship to Him. Furthermore, I am convinced that this choice is one that we must make deliberately, and daily. This decision is the key to putting Jesus first in our lives.

Choice has brought great blessing and direction to my life. During my daily prayer walk, I tell God that I am choosing that day to walk, think, speak, dream, and lead in the fear of the Lord. I believe this practice has resulted in great blessings and clearer direction for my life. It has truly helped me to live for Christ first.

"E" STANDS FOR "EXPRESS YOURSELF IN AN HONEST AND TRANSPARENT MANNER"

Simply put, be truthful and open in communication with God and others. Listen to what the Scriptures teach us about these character qualities:

May my spoken words and unspoken thoughts be pleasing even to you, O Lord my Rock and my Redeemer.

—PSALM 19:14, TLB

For, "Whoever would love life and see good days must keep his tongue from evil and his lips from deceitful speech."

—1 PETER 3:10, NIV

Truthful lips endure forever, but a lying tongue lasts only a moment.

—PROVERBS 12:19, NIV

Honesty and transparency in leadership are indispensable to effectively discussing behavior and performance issues that may arise with your team members. Too often, leaders avoid honest dialogue with subordinates, shirking their responsibility to provide meaningful feedback. In my experience, though, constructive criticism finds far more acceptance when those receiving it know their leaders both care about them and have no hidden agendas.

Clearly state your expectations. Not doing so can lead to confusion, frustration, and discouragement. Such employees or colleagues then find themselves in an impossible situation: They have no clear idea of what they are to do, yet may feel they continually fall short in your eyes. It is as if they are locked inside their leader's prison of expectations. The truth, told with honesty and transparency, can set them free to achieve!

Further, being honest about my own mistakes has opened the door for me to give honest feedback to others. In fact, I have painfully discovered that if you are *not* honest and transparent when you share with others, they will not trust you. Oh, they may never tell you that to your face, but you can be sure they will tell everyone else about their mistrust for you as a leader.

"A" STANDS FOR "ADVANCE TOWARD YOUR PROBLEMS AND GOALS"

Bear experts will tell you the worst thing you can do when confronted by a grizzly is to run. Instead, they advise standing your ground, making noise with pots and pans, and even shouting. No human being—not even an Olympic gold medalist sprinter—can outrun a bear! The same is true when problems arise on your leadership horizon.

Indeed, rather than running away or ignoring such challenges, I have learned to run *toward* the problem! Consider this scripture:

> Brethren, I do not count myself to have apprehended; but one thing I do, forgetting those things which are behind and reaching forward to those things which are ahead, I press toward the goal for the prize of the upward call of God in Christ Jesus.
>
> —PHILIPPIANS 3:13–14

After some tough lessons early in my leadership life, I learned that facing problems with colleagues and those under my authority may be painful or stressful in the short run, but avoiding potential conflict just makes things worse. Issues don't go away by dodging them; they can be like untreated wounds, festering into serious, spreading infections.

Are you facing such an issue? Ask God the following questions: *How can I run toward this problem? Lord, what are some practical steps I can take? Lord, is there someone who might be able to help me or who has faced this problem before?*

If you ask God these sorts of questions, He promises to help you:

> If you need wisdom—if you want to know what God wants you to do—ask Him, and He will gladly tell you. He will not resent your asking.
>
> —JAMES 1:5, TLB

In addition to that wisdom, I have also found it helpful to thank God for the courage to move toward whatever problems arise.

Along with that courage to forge ahead, pray that your goals are God's goals. I am convinced that God will only bless our advance toward goals—designs, ambitions, objectives, etc.—that He has given us. The Lord has a plan for each one of our lives; if we are open to His voice, He will share the goals that move us toward fulfilling our unique, God-drafted life blueprint:

> For we are God's masterpiece. He has created us anew in Christ Jesus, so we can do the good things he planned for us long ago.
>
> —EPHESIANS 2:10, NLT

God uses goals to help us grow and to motivate change within us and those we connect with day to day. I have also discovered that striving toward His goals can take us places we never dreamed, just as dropping a pebble in a pond can send ripples to the farthest shore. His goals for our lives—our potential in His hands—are always bigger than what we could ever accomplish on our own.

Talk with the Lord about the goals He has for you. Be open to His

lesigns, purposes, and blessings for your life, and ask Him
..em to you. Here is a question and some principles unleashed
..ing it that have helped me discover God's direction in my life:

*God, what can I do right now to start moving toward this
goal?*

Asking the question is also a statement of commitment and
submission on my part. From that point, I have learned that:

1. God usually gives me small steps of faith to take toward
   the goal.

2. He gives me the grace to take those steps.

3. He does not unveil His enabling power until I take the
   first step He has shown me.

4. He values persistence. In other words, don't give up on
   a goal just because it seems impossible!

"D" Stands for "Determine to Be a Servant to Both Those Over and Under You"

A leader is first and foremost a servant. Listen to some powerful
instruction from Jesus on this key principle:

> "Whoever wants to become great among you must be your ser-
> vant, and whoever wants to be first must be your slave—just
> as the Son of Man did not come to be served, but to serve, and
> to give his life as a ransom for many."
>
> —Matthew 20:26–28, niv

> "The greatest among you will be your servant. For whoever
> exalts himself will be humbled, and whoever humbles himself
> will be exalted."
>
> —Matthew 23:11–12, niv

I believe there is a spiritual law related to leadership and responsibility: As our leadership and responsibilities increase, God expects us
to become greater servants.

Leadership is all about being faithful servants. As leaders, we need to embrace the attitude of putting our subordinates' needs first. As subordinates, we are called to serve in the same way toward our bosses. Sound confusing? It's not, really. Consider that if either your boss or those under your authority look good, *you* look good.

So, ask God for a servant's heart. We have Christ's example and His word that He will promote people whose lives resound with the heartbeat of Jesus.

Taking this approach of being servant to *both* superiors and subordinates alike can raise some eyebrows, so be prepared for that. An example of this comes from my next to last assignment for the military, as Director of Contracting for the Air Force Space and Missile Systems Center. One day, I was having a conversation with my executive officer, a young man I came to value as a friend as well as a trusted right-hand man. (Indeed, later, as a pastor, I officiated at his wedding.) "So, Brian, what's the scuttlebutt out there?" It was an inquiry I regularly made, wanting to stay on top of what was happening in my organization. I counted on my "XO" to be my finger on the pulse of a directorate with several hundred military and civilian employees and multimillion-dollar responsibilities.

Well, this trusted officer shared this and that, then almost floored me with this comment: "Sir, they call you the 'weird colonel' out there."

I didn't quite know what to think of that. I didn't initially take it as a compliment!

Seeing my reaction etched on my face, Brian quickly added: "Colonel Johnson, it's really a good thing. You don't behave as the typical colonel, is what they mean. They feel you are there to serve them, that you really care about them!"

I decided he was right; this *was* a good thing. This "weird colonel" stood out because he didn't rule with a closed mind and iron fist. The way I had decided to lead—the way the Lord had led me to lead—hopefully made my subordinates want to follow. So, I had to smile; this echoed what I felt when my own superiors had shown interest in my ideas and my life and career, too.

"E" Stands for "Expect God to Use You to Impact Others"

At the deepest core of the Christian leader's heart is the desire to impact the lives of others, or at least it should be. I pray every day for God to affect others positively through me. This is what Jesus lived for, and He told us to do the same. He gives us His Holy Spirit power and builds the needed character qualities in us to fulfill this mission.

But I believe we must ask and expect that God will use us. James, a first-century church leader who many Bible scholars believe was the stepbrother of Jesus, put it this way:

> If you want to know what God wants you to do, ask him, and he will gladly tell you, for he is always ready to give a bountiful supply of wisdom to all who ask him; he will not resent it. But when you ask him, be sure that you really expect him to tell you, for a doubtful mind will be as unsettled as a wave of the sea that is driven and tossed by the wind; and every decision you then make will be uncertain, as you turn first this way and then that. If you don't ask with faith, don't expect the Lord to give you any solid answer.
>
> —James 1:5–7, tlb

The Apostle John wrote this in his gospel:

> "I tell you the truth, anyone who has faith in me will do what I have been doing. He will do even greater things than these, because I am going to the Father. And I will do whatever you ask in my name, so that the Son may bring glory to the Father. You may ask me for anything in my name, and I will do it."
>
> —John 14:12–14, niv

Those seem to be pretty clear instructions from our Lord. It seems certain that God not only wants to use me to make a big impact for His kingdom, but He wants to use others in the same way. Still, we often falter when it comes to believing God could use us. Or we may believe that for others but not for ourselves.

When you have such doubts, it is time to shift your perspective—to remember it is not about us; it is all about God working *through us*. It is a simple truth: God has chosen to use men and women to bring His salvation, healing, power, and provision to this sad, suffering Earth. *Ask and expect God to use you!* Then don't be surprised when He does just that.

In 1999, I met with a two-star general in the Pentagon. This man was a fine leader and mentor to me, and we had developed a bond of mutual respect. This conversation came at a crossroads late in my Air Force career. My current director's position was to be replaced with a civilian manager; I was being pushed toward moving on to another posting or to retire after what was then a twenty-seven-year stint in the military.

That day, I talked with the general about his promotion to oversee all the big Department of Defense and National Aeronautics and Space Administration (NASA) contracts both in the US and overseas. He had just gotten the job and would be taking on his new duties in a few months.

"Stu, what are you going to do?" he suddenly asked, aware of my situation. I told him I would like to stay in the Air Force if I was given a challenging position; otherwise, I was considering retirement.

The general eyed me for a moment, then seemed to make a decision. "If I made you commander of the Western United States in my organization, would you do that?" he asked.

As his subordinate commander, I would be leading almost six thousand people, including nineteen other colonels and twelve lieutenant colonels from not just the Air Force but similar ranking officers in the Army, Navy, and Marine Corps. We would be responsible for managing contracts worth billions of taxpayer dollars. The pressure of this job could be enormous.

But I felt strongly this offer was from the Lord. And as I said, "Yes, I would do that," I felt a peaceful witness within my spirit. At least, I did until after the meeting concluded and I was a few steps outside the general's office.

Suddenly, as the challenges ahead flooded into my mind, I thought, "God, what have I just done?" I fought off the panic and prayed for the same wisdom God had granted young, frightened King Solomon millennia ago:

"Now give me wisdom and knowledge, that I may go out and come in before this people; for who can judge this great people of Yours?"

—2 Chronicles 1:10

The Lord answered Solomon's prayer, and He was just as faithful in answering mine. After I had been in that new job just a month, the general said he had never seen someone learn to navigate a command so quickly or discover where to focus their leadership. I thanked him for saying that but credited the success he saw as an answer to prayer.

God wants to use us to impact others, but first we must expect Him to do so. Often, that means trusting Him as you take the first step—and then asking for and counting on Him to provide you the wisdom for the steps that follow.

"R" Stands for "Respond Positively When Problems Arise"

You will need that wisdom you prayed for to handle the problems that inevitably rise like mountains before you in whatever arena of leadership is yours. God promises us that wisdom—that knowledge of what is true or right, combined with just judgment—and the power to overcome obstacles:

Jesus replied, "I tell you the truth, if you have faith and do not doubt, not only can you do what was done to the fig tree, but also you can say to this mountain, 'Go, throw yourself into the sea,' and it will be done. If you believe, you will receive whatever you ask for in prayer."

—Matthew 21:21–22, NIV

The Apostle Paul offered these words of encouragement:

I can do all things through Christ who strengthens me.

—Philippians 4:13

The one who calls you is faithful and he will do it.

—1 Thessalonians 5:24, NIV

God powerfully uses problems in our lives to show His faithfulness to us, to grow our faith, and to speak to those around us that there is a God who cares and responds. Do you have problems? Of course. We all do. Look at them as opportunities to make things better, to correct bad policy and practices, to involve and teach people, and to make you and others stronger!

When someone comes to you with problems, don't shoot the messenger. Listen, and go a step further: Teach your subordinates (and yourself) to bring along their best recommendations for a solution to the problems they find. Do that, and you nurture the attitude of turning problems into opportunities for your staff and eventually your entire organization.

REFLECTIONS

Does Jesus have first place in your life? What would other people—your church, your family, and your friends—say if asked that about you? What kind of grade do you give yourself?

How do you express yourself to others? Are you honest with people? Are you transparent? Does your tone express caring? *Do you run toward your problems and goals?* Do you have a problem you are hoping will go away? Are you taking godly steps toward your goals?

Do you really expect God to use you? Do you have some current examples? Remember, it is not about you; it is all about Him.

How do you react to problems? Do you see opportunities or just trouble? Do you shoot "problem" messengers?

Chapter Two

THE ATTITUDE OF THE LEADER

ATTITUDE. ANOTHER WORD for it could be *perspective*. It is our spiritual, emotional, and mental perspective on and disposition about life, circumstances, and people. Attitude can be negative or positive. Either way, as a Christian leader, your attitude comprises your starting point in any relationship, whether that is with someone in authority over you or with someone under your authority.

Winston Churchill was a leader recognized by history for carrying—with grit and determination—the war-weary, battered British people through the darkest days of World War II to victory over Hitler's Nazis. Churchill also had quite the dry, wry, and yet piercing wit. "Attitude is a little thing that makes a big difference," this beloved prime minister once said.

The New Testament offers even more powerful advice directed to Christians in leadership. Listen to these words from the Apostle Paul:

> Don't fret or worry. Instead of worrying, pray. Let petitions and praises shape your worries into prayer, letting God know your concerns. Before you know it, a sense of God's wholeness, everything coming together for good, will settle you down. It's wonderful when Christ displaces worry at the center of your life.
>
> Summing it all up, friends, I'd say you'll do best by filling your minds and meditating on things true, noble, reputable, authentic, compelling, gracious—the best, not the worst; the beautiful, not the ugly; things to praise, not to curse.
> —PHILIPPIANS 4:6–8, THE MESSAGE

Talk about a handbook for proper attitude in a spiritual nutshell! I am convinced that it is our attitude, and not just our abilities, that ultimately determines most of what we achieve in our lives. If our attitude is positive, we give God fertile ground to work in us, through us, and around us.

At its core, attitude is a choice we make in how we will look at and respond to life. Indeed, it is amazing to me how that choice, for good or ill, can even affect how a person sees and interprets facts!

A bad attitude can even lead you to dispute something that, viewed honestly, is really indisputable. All of us can recall such a person (perhaps even ourselves, at times) whose perspective was so twisted by a negative attitude that they could look out a window of the orbiting space shuttle and *still* insist the Earth was flat!

The saying is true: "Attitude is everything." I also like the way College Football Hall of Fame coach Lou Holtz once expanded on that idea: "Ability is what you're capable of doing. Motivation determines what you do. Attitude determines how well you do it."

Your choices will establish the kind of attitude you have. Here are seven components I have found make up a winning, positive attitude. Each of them requires important choices—decisions that are critical to building a godly leadership attitude.

Choose to Believe God Is in Control

The Bible is chock full of this assurance. God's ultimate control is at the foundation of trust, and trusting God is the DNA of a vibrant, Christian faith. One scripture verse in particular has been helpful in planting this theme in my mind and heart:

> He has put all things in subjection under His feet.
> —Ephesians 1:22, NASB

God the Father has given His Son, Jesus Christ, authority over everything. Jesus is in charge, not you or me. It will be God's purposes which ultimately prevail, not yours or mine.

If your attitude is poisoning your faith and trust in God's sovereignty, you will worry, become anxiety-ridden, and perhaps even have a nervous breakdown. What good will that do you? We are out of control; God, our all-wise, all-loving and eternally trustworthy Lord, is in control of everything!

During my Air Force career, there was an all-too-popular phrase used to describe a leader who was out of control, or just plain worried, impatient, angry, selfish, and miserable to work for: "He's running around with his hair on fire!" Often I or my fellow officers would ask, "How is the boss today?" Too often, the answer was that he or she was figuratively darting here and there with smoke rolling off his or her head.

Now, you would think Christians would be far less inclined to be galloping around with their metaphorical hair afire. Sadly, if you look at any congregation—and especially the leadership of that church—well, let's just say that if there was such a thing as a spiritual worry- and stress-activated fire suppression sprinkler system, a lot of our church leaders would be drenched!

All this anxiety from trying to control our circumstances instead of taking our hands off the steering wheel of life and letting God drive not only is guaranteed to end in defeat, but it makes those around us miserable, too. I've been there myself and have learned the hard way to remember this truth: My present circumstances are not the final chapter of what God is doing in my life.

God's Word tells us:

> And we know that all things work together for good to those who love God, to those who are the called according to His purpose.
>
> —ROMANS 8:28

At a church where I was one of the leaders, we ran into a particularly vexing problem with a couple in a volunteer ministry position. A conflict had erupted that, like a whirlpool in a river, eventually drew in one lay leader after another on opposing sides. It became clear that this couple, particularly the wife, was the catalyst for this. We met with her and her husband in an effort to settle the issue.

Unfortunately, her response was to escalate the situation, even attempting to draw in other leaders outside our church. An oppressive spirit settled over our congregation like a cloud of choking smog.

It was like someone had taken a torch and thrown it into our church. Leaders felt the situation was out of control. One night, as I walked on our patio and thought and prayed about this mess, I realized this was

God's situation to control, and finally I laid it at His feet. When I did, I was flooded by a sense of peace. I knew the Lord would handle it.

I shared my new sense of peace with the other leaders. The Lord then moved through that group. You could see the peace smooth furrowed brows, and those who had been on the fence in the conflict had new resolve and a sense that things were going to work for good.

Things turned around when we allowed the Holy Spirit to lead us out of our fruitless efforts to control the crisis and put it on the altar before God. Our hands, which had been so busy trying to fix this escalating situation, were then empty and ready to do the work the Lord had called us to do.

I smile now, remembering how I paced that patio until I heard the Lord tell us in my spirit: "I am in control. If you want to take control, go ahead. However, if you do, the circumstances will only get worse." At that time, though, there was nothing amusing about it at all. I felt deeply convicted about my attitude.

Now, painful as that situation was, I thank God for it! Once we had repented of our attitudes and remembered who was in charge—God— things came to a resolution that reunited our church and got us back on track as His children.

Join me now in declaring aloud, "I choose to believe that God is in control."

CHOOSE TO FILL YOUR MIND WITH GOD'S THOUGHTS

Again, in a different arena—that of the mind—it is all about *control.* Before God can pour His thinking into your being, you have to make room in that cluttered closet of a brain so many of us have. The Apostle Paul certainly knew all about this second component of the godly leader's attitude:

> For the weapons of our warfare are not carnal but mighty in God for pulling down strongholds, casting down arguments and every high thing that exalts itself against the knowledge of God, bringing every thought into captivity to the obedience of Christ.
>
> —2 CORINTHIANS 10:4–5

15

God expects us to control our thought life. *What?* Yes. He wants us to develop self-discipline to bring our thinking under rein. Of course, that is quite the challenge, isn't it? Oh, I admit it is not easy for me to control my thought life—but I have also learned that life gets a lot harder if I do not do so.

That is because of the chain reaction thoughts can bring, for good or bad. Thoughts lead to words; words lead to actions; actions lead to habits; and habits influence my destiny.

I have found four steps helpful in keeping my thoughts under control. First, I need to turn off the "movies" I play in my mind. Mind movies are those imaginary situations, conversations, and observations we so often allow to take over our thoughts.

Here's an example. Perhaps I begin an imaginary conversation in my mind with a person I'm having difficulty with in some aspect of my life. As I allow that confrontation to build, it morphs from whimsy into real feelings. Pretty soon, my emotions are all stirred up and my heart is beating faster—and several minutes of my real life have been wasted.

Imagination is a gift from God, but like anything, it can be twisted onto dark paths our Lord doesn't want us getting lost following. When that happens, imagination takes over, and it can be a hard-to-resist taskmaster. Before a thought stream goes too far, ask God to forgive you the moment you realize your mind movie has pulled you away from His purposes. Then, consciously—out loud, if that works better for you—give control of your thoughts back to Him, and thank Him for the strength and desire to change course.

The second step toward controlling your thoughts comes the moment you begin to worry. Instead of allowing your imagination to fire up the projector again—this time a horror flick featuring your fears—use worry as a cue to start praying. For me, it is really that simple. As soon as I realize I have allowed worry to crowd out my trust in God, I pray.

Here's what the Bible advises:

> Don't worry about anything; instead, pray about everything.
> Tell God what you need, and thank him for all he has done.
> Then you will experience God's peace, which exceeds anything

we can understand. His peace will guard your hearts and minds as you live in Christ Jesus.

—PHILIPPIANS 4:6–7, NLT

The third step? I try to control my "dead time." Dead time is when my mind can easily lose focus. I know that my thoughts can easily wander when I am driving, taking a walk, or sitting in an airport. Your dead times may be different. I have tried to specifically use these times for focused prayer.

During an assignment in Washington, DC, for example, I had a forty-five-minute drive to work every day. My mind used to wander during this drive, worrying about the operation I had inherited, one crippled by poor morale and office infighting. As a result, I often arrived at work anxious and uptight. After a few months of wasting this valuable time, I realized that God had given me the gift of valuable time in the car to pray. Controlling what had previously been dead time dramatically impacted my life. I arrived at work refreshed and ready to hit the ground running.

Fourth, instead of filling my mind with those movies and worry, I've learned it is much more profitable to fill it with Scripture. Find some Bible verses that speak to where you are in your life. Memorize them; think about what they mean; use them in your prayers to God. God's Word has a way of changing our perspective and redeeming our thoughts!

Pause right now and say, "I choose daily to fill my mind with God's thoughts."

CHOOSE TO SPEAK POSITIVELY ABOUT OTHERS

This third component of a winning, God-honored attitude is incredibly important—and it is one of the easiest to violate; it goes contrary to our selfish, fallen nature, after all. But speaking positively about others is nothing less than a command direct from the Word of God:

Don't criticize and speak evil about each other, dear brothers.

—JAMES 4:11, TLB

And this:

> Say only what is good and helpful to those you are talking to,
> and what will give them a blessing.
>
> —Ephesians 4:29, tlb

One of the most effective, immediate steps to take in your determination to speak only positively about others is refusing to share, or even listen to gossip and rumors. That's a tough one for many Christians, who latch onto the latest gossip or spread rumors under the guise of prayer requests. Or, we say we are "concerned…in love" with the conduct or accusations (often groundless) against a brother or sister in the faith.

Gossip and the church rumor mill crank up to full speed when the target is a pastor or other church leader. And unfortunately, leaders themselves seem to fall prey to temptation to pass on a juicy tidbit, dressed up in spiritual vernacular. I believe a good rule, especially for those in leadership, is to never share anything with another person unless he or she is part of the solution or absolutely needs to know the information being shared.

It also follows, then, that we should never listen to information about another person unless *we* are part of the solution to a problem or an integral part of the situation.

Choosing to speak positively about others also means we should not assume we know others' motives. Think about it. If you are like me, you don't get angry or judgmental about what others say and do; those reactions jump out of your mind and onto your lips because of what you think was behind what they did. So often, we assume motives behind people's actions and words—and I have found that when I do that, I'm usually wrong.

My batting average for such assumptions has been awful, in fact. I cannot count the times I have been wrong in this area. Now, if I get upset with someone's actions or words, I make it a rule to ask *why* they did or said what they did. Often their answer changes my entire perspective!

Here's another hard-won lesson I've learned about trying to speak only positively about others: My first impressions of subordinates, colleagues, and my own superiors—whether in secular service or the ministry—has almost always been wrong.

As I have worked with people and gotten to know them better, generally my assessment of their skills, character, and potential get adjusted upward. First impressions should never be allowed to take root in your mental archives; they are anything but absolute and *never* should be the basis for judgments or decisions involving others.

Finally, choosing to speak positively about others means we must never pass sentence on others. What I mean by that term is the all-too-human tendency to quickly pigeonhole others—to label people, for example, as stupid, rude, insensitive, selfish, etc.

For any honest and serious Christian, it should be abundantly apparent that it just is not our business to exercise such snap judgments and mentally dismiss another child of God. At its heart, this practice is really just an excuse for our own insensitivity and lack of caring!

As a young believer, I learned this truth the hard way. I developed a serious attitude problem regarding a worship leader. I didn't care for the song selections—a lot of hymns, and not many of the newer, upbeat choruses. Or I thought the leader was too loud, too rushed, too whatever. For me, there was no shortage of choices, styles, or abilities to criticize. In my heart, I judged the person as a poor fit for worship leadership.

Then one night after an evening service, this leader came up to me and asked if I would pray for a particular need.

I smugly headed into a back room to pray. But when I opened my mouth, I blurted out, "I want to ask your forgiveness for being so critical of you!"

I was probably as surprised—well, more so—than the leader was. That was an involuntary confession on my part; the Holy Spirit had taken over, and once I heard my own words, my heart broke. I realized in a flash that I had been wrong, and that, willingly or not, initially, those were *exactly* the words I needed to share. The smug attitude I had begun with was broken; I asked forgiveness.

But my surprises were not done that night. "Stu, I want to ask for your forgiveness," the leader said, "because I've been very critical of you, too."

We began right there on the road to a deep friendship. We shared our lives—our hopes, dreams, fears, and challenges—and prayed for each other. From then on, my critical spirit melted away; I didn't notice or care about those little things that had bothered me before.

Now, I better knew the person; I even became a defender of this leader. When someone would sidle up to me with a critical comment about this person, my response was, "No, I didn't see that." Then I would add, "You know, I love this person."

Judgment and criticism had been replaced with love and respect. The Holy Spirit had taught me that night that you just don't know someone until you hear his or her story!

I wish now that before I allowed myself to fall into such a critical frame of mind, I had read and taken to heart this scripture:

> Therefore judge nothing before the appointed time; wait till the Lord comes. He will bring to light what is hidden in darkness and will expose the motives of men's hearts. At that time each will receive his praise from God.
> —1 Corinthians 4:5, niv

God is the judge, and He does not need my help or yours.

Pause right now and say with me: "I choose to speak positively about others."

Choose to Be a Thankful Person

By this point in our journey toward building a blessed leadership attitude, we have declared that God is in control; we have determined to exercise the mental and spiritual discipline to fill our minds with God's thoughts; and we have made a commitment to speak positively about others. Now we add to those components the choice to be a thankful person—to not just feel gratitude but to internalize it to the point where it overflows into the way we speak, interact with others, and approach both blessings and setbacks.

Jesus certainly found that a thankful person is an attractive person; so do other people. I love this story from the Bible, which is a beautiful illustration of this point:

> Now it happened as He went to Jerusalem that He passed through the midst of Samaria and Galilee. Then as He entered

a certain village, there met Him ten men who were lepers, who stood afar off. And they lifted up their voices and said, "Jesus, Master, have mercy on us!"

So when He saw them, He said to them, "Go, show yourselves to the priests." And so it was that as they went, they were cleansed.

And one of them, when he saw that he was healed, returned, and with a loud voice glorified God, and fell down on his face at His feet, giving Him thanks. And he was a Samaritan.

So Jesus answered and said, "Were there not ten cleansed? But where are the nine?"

—LUKE 17:11–17

Those ten lepers could easily represent people in general, don't you think? If so, then do only 10 percent of us show any gratitude to God or others on a consistent basis? In fact, interacting with the mass of humanity out there on a given day, do you think that even 10 percent fall into the thankful camp?

Of course, it is not the right attitude to do things for people in hopes of harvesting praise or thanks from them. Still, we all will admit that hearing an occasional "thank you" can be very encouraging.

Years ago, I got into the practice of periodically sending out personal birthday notes to my subordinates. The impact initially stunned me; I had recipients coming up to me with tears in their eyes. This simple act of heartfelt recognition took a few minutes of my time, but you would have thought I'd written them a check for a million dollars rather than a simple little note!

This revelation truly had humble, slightly desperate beginnings. Previously, I had simply sent out birthday cards to people in my organization; I'd write a brief greeting on it, mail it off, and I was done. But the time came when my staff included three hundred fifty people and thirty commanders. I was living in Los Angeles at the time, the kids were in college, and finances were stretched...and cards—that many, at least—were expensive.

My solution was to handwrite each person a note on my official stationary. What was something of an expedient for me—though the messages were indeed from the heart—were seen as far more thoughtful than the cards!

Afterward, as I mused over the overwhelmingly positive reception the notes had garnered, I had to chuckle. I wished I had known this sooner; it would have saved me a lot of money, for one, but more importantly, I would have touched more of my subordinates in a meaningful way.

Being a thankful person means three things to me.

One, *I am quick to thank others for helping me.* The operative word here is *quick.* The effect of a "thank you" loses its emotional (and I would argue, spiritual) sweetness in time—just like a ripe tomato, left on the vine day after day, soon turns moldy. If your "thank you" comes days or weeks late, the words lose their power. They become a meaningless afterthought.

Two, *I express thanksgiving in my daily prayers.* The Scriptures resound with this principle. Here is just one of them, a favorite of mine:

> Enter his gates with thanksgiving and his courts with praise;
> give thanks to him and praise his name.
>
> —Psalm 100:4, NIV

Think of it this way: Thanksgiving gets you in the door, and praise brings you into God's presence.

The Johnson family periodically takes time before God dedicated to only offering prayers of thanks. It is amazing what changes in attitude this can bring and what enhancement to a family's sense of well-being will come as a result. And that sort of attitude also opens your family to the Lord's blessings—and more to be thankful for!

This same approach applies beyond the family unit, of course. Such times of devoted thankfulness in prayer works wonders within your pastoral staff, your church board, and within a congregation as a whole. Whether thanks and praise come from one mouth or many, attitudes are changed and blessings result.

Three, *I do not behave as if the world owes me something.* Essentially, such behavior is birthed in an attitude of ingratitude.

In one of my assignments, a wonderful Christian woman worked for me. Her position was not considered especially "high grade" in the traditional organizational chart. But she volunteered as the organizer of social events, like picnics, luncheons, etc. Her professionalism in the office and unselfish, hard work outside of it had earned the respect of her co-workers and her superiors. She had a positive impact far beyond her assigned duties.

However, one day I noticed she seemed uncharacteristically somber and withdrawn during a meeting, so I hung around afterward and took her aside to talk. "How are you doing?" I asked, noting that she seemed to have something weighing heavily upon her. As I learned, it wasn't just a heavy burden. It was a crushing one.

The story she told me was soul-rending. She lived in a tough section of the city, and her son had gotten in with a bad crowd. He had been involved in a robbery, arrested, and jailed. While incarcerated, for reasons unknown, he had been killed by another inmate. Understandably, she was struggling. She was bitter toward the police, the courts, and of course the jail, and she was angry with God about it all.

As she cried and poured out her heart, my own broke. We ended the meeting with prayer, after which she went back to her duties.

But her story didn't end in that state. A couple weeks later, I bumped into her again—and what a change! Her face radiated joy, not the strain of grief, loss, and rage. Of course, I asked her what had happened to so change her attitude.

As tragic as her earlier account had been, this new one was gloriously triumphant. One evening, she and her husband were watching television. Something caught her eye, and she looked into the room's entryway—*and saw an angel.*

This being from heaven had a simple message for her: *You need to forgive those involved in your son's death. You need to let go of your bitterness and start thanking God.*

Thanking God? For what? She soon found out, after she obeyed and her attitude lightened. Not long after that, she and her husband (who was not a believer) were watching TV again when a Christian music program came on. Instead of switching channels, though, he seemed riveted.

Right in the middle of the program, he suddenly gave his life to Christ. His wife's thankful attitude—despite every human reason to feel the opposite—had provided fertile ground for God's blessings.

Pause right now and say with me, "I choose to be a thankful person."

Choose to Forgive and to Ask Forgiveness Quickly

The Word of God has many spiritual themes and lessons to teach, but the one underlying this entire account of our heavenly Father's history with His human creations rides on one prime principle and gift beyond comprehension: the unfathomable love the Lord has shown us in His forgiveness. He requires that this elemental part of His nature find a home in our hearts. Forgiveness is a virtue we *must* embrace and practice, or we are lost. Period.

> Forgive one another as quickly and thoroughly as God in Christ forgave you.
>
> —Ephesians 4:32, the message

Think of this as a race that tests your spiritual character, and not a nice, slow jog or a marathon where you pace yourself over a long distance, either. Forgiveness is a sprint. This is a race God expects us to run with a leap out of the starting blocks, full out; a second- or third-place finish won't do. It is a race He wants us to win.

This is especially true for leaders in His kingdom because they set an example for those they serve. I learned an important lesson in this as a father, perhaps the most elemental leadership position there is.

One night, after a particularly tiring day, I came home, only to blow up at my little boy. He was three or four years old at the time. I cannot today even remember what set me off specifically, but I spoke harshly to him. Immediately, my heavenly Father let me have it. Conviction came like a lightning bolt, and inside my mind, that still, small voice of His rebuked me: "You go back to him now. You kneel down to your son's height, look him in the eye, and ask him to forgive you!"

Broken, I did just that. I looked in those little eyes, told him I was sorry, and asked him to forgive me. He reached out his tiny hand and touched me on the forehead and said, "Daddy, it's OK." It was just a few words he spoke, but what was in this child's gaze spoke volumes more. In my son's eyes, I felt like I had grown. He already loved me, but that look seemed to say, "Daddy, you are really something special!"

How about you? Be first to ask forgiveness. Set the example. Leaders *lead*. Leaders go first! Don't wait for the right opportunity. Do it *now*.

What's the best time to ask forgiveness? *As soon as you realize you have done wrong.* And here's the miracle: Forgiveness not only begins the healing in you, the offender, but also within the offended.

Someone has to take the first step, though. Leaders take that first step!

Pause right now and say with me, "I choose to forgive and ask forgiveness quickly."

CHOOSE TO BE A PROBLEM-SOLVER AND NOT A WHINER

Remember this verse from earlier in this book? Paul shared priceless wisdom he had learned from the Lord that beautifully applies to this point:

> One thing I do, forgetting those things which are behind and reaching forward to those things which are ahead, I press toward the goal for the prize of the upward call of God in Christ Jesus.
>
> —PHILIPPIANS 3:13–14

If you want to solve problems, don't look where you have already been. Reach forward to grasp those challenges with both hands. It comes down to this. There are really just two things you can do when a problem looms on your horizon. First, and this is most often what we do, we can whine about our lot and the impossibility of the situation. Or second, and this is the path to victory, we can solve the problems we face by calling upon God's strength and wisdom.

Over the last decade I served as an Air Force officer, I reserved a prominent space on my office wall for a sign—one that both reminded me of what my own attitude should be toward problems and suggested the same to any visitors. It simply read: "Thou Shalt Not Whine." I called it the eleventh commandment. I tried to obey it, and I asked my staff to do the same.

It's not any fun to be around someone who constantly whines about pretty much everything unpleasant that comes into his or her life. We all know that. But choosing to be a problem-solver is more than a matter of civility. It means you determine to focus on solutions, not bemoaning the latest roadblock that inevitably appears just around the curve on everyone's journey.

A secretary once gave me some good advice. She was a single mother trying to make it in a very expensive city. Now there was a woman who had plenty of reasons to whine! But she refused to allow that attitude of defeat to infect her or her children.

"I allow myself and my children fifteen seconds of whining each day," she told me. "This usually takes place at the breakfast table, and no further whining is allowed. It has made our home much happier!"

A story is told of two veterans in the hospital recovering from serious war wounds. Whether these heroes would survive and recover was up in the air. One of these men had a bed next to the window, while the other was located on the opposite wall without a view outside.

The patient at the window started describing to his roommate what he saw. He did this day after day, doing his best to encourage his comrade-in-arms.

Actually, though, this all had the opposite effect. The man away from the window view became more discontent each day. Instead of appreciating his roommate's efforts, he grew to resent them, growing increasingly bitter. Then one day, the veteran at the window died, and the surviving patient got his wish: He was moved to the spot near the window.

But when he took a look with his own eyes outside this coveted portal, he was startled to see that instead of the flowers, trees, people, and other things his deceased roommate had described, there was only the brick wall of another section of the hospital. His now-dead friend had used his imagination in an effort to make their days more bearable, more beautiful. Instead of whining about his window opening onto a drab brick wall, the man had chosen to invite creativity and life into that sad and sterile space.

The single character flaw of whining can stain and weaken the effectiveness of anyone, even if they are top-notch in every other area of their lives. That was the case of a man who once worked for me.

This fellow was a tremendous leader in so many ways. He was bright, extremely creative, a good leader, and very caring toward his people. But he also was a whiner at times. He would send excruciatingly long e-mails about an issue or situation that easily could have been described in a sentence or two.

It got to where everyone who worked with him would laugh about his proclivity for these mini-novels. He turned out to be the inspiration, so to speak, for a gift his organization gave me when I left my job there: an animated, stuffed toy chicken that would emit a whining cackle while flapping its wings and kicking its legs.

I kept that chicken in my new office for many years, activating it whenever one of the staff got carried away with whining about this or that. It proved to be a low-key, humorous, yet effective way to get the message across. But that was not the chicken's last duty for its country.

During peacekeeping missions to Bosnia, my organization oversaw the contractor workforce, providing the care and feeding of those soldiers charged with enforcing order and keeping the warring parties away from each other. As mission demands increased and military budgets got tighter, more of these support roles were taken out of military hands and put under civilian contractors. It was part of my job, every six months, to dispatch fifty-member teams to oversee those non-military employees and make sure they fulfilled their responsibilities.

The strain and demands finally got to one of these units. Toward the end of its mission, the team simply imploded. Long deployments can wear down the best of us, and that's what happened in this case. Living in tents, away from loved ones, in the middle of groups of people whose hate for each other has simmered for centuries, minor interpersonal irritations became major personnel problems.

I knew I had to find a way to prevent this from happening again, or the mission itself would begin to unravel. My solution? Special orders for the chicken. The whining beast went out with the next team to Bosnia with these orders from me: "Guys, when you start getting irritated and you sense the urge to whine coming on, pull out and activate the chicken. Then have a healthy team meeting to air your grievances."

Seems pretty silly, doesn't it? But that chicken, flapping its wings, kicking its feet, and cackling in outrage, did its job. In fact, it did its job so well in relieving pressure and sparking positive interaction that, to my surprise, it got a nice, fat promotion.

When that particular unit returned from its six-month stint in Bosnia, the chicken came back as a newly-minted "colonel"—bearing my nametag and wearing its own custom-made camouflage uniform! That chicken went on more tours in Bosnia, keeping one team after another on an even emotional keel. This literal "bird colonel" became quite famous!

Once you stop laughing, pause with me and say, "I choose to be a problem-solver, not a whiner."

CHOOSE TO MAKE EVERY PERSON YOU MEET AND EVERY PLACE YOU GO BETTER BECAUSE OF CHRIST IN YOU

This is not only the final component of a godly leader's attitude, it is the point of our service! Of course, it is the Spirit of the Lord that makes people and places better, but God also has chosen to do much of this work through men and women. It is a special privilege, and an awesome responsibility, to be called upon to influence and touch so many people this way.

Here is what Jesus had to say about it:

> "You are the salt of the earth; but if the salt loses its flavor, how shall it be seasoned? It is then good for nothing but to be thrown out and trampled underfoot by men.
>
> "You are the light of the world. A city that is set on a hill cannot be hidden. Nor do they light a lamp and put it under a basket, but on a lamp stand, and it gives light to all who are in the house. Let your light so shine before men, that they may see your good works and glorify your Father in heaven."
>
> —MATTHEW 5:13–16

No matter what your calling or ministry within the kingdom of God may be, as a Christian leader, you have been gifted with a platform from which to impact the lives of many people. It helps to have a personal way to remind ourselves of that reality.

I have found these affirmations helpful. Say them, believe them, and confess them:

- I am God's ambassador.

- God wants to use me, and I will cooperate with Him.

- God wants me to share His love and redemption.

- I am honored to bring His presence and power to every person I meet and every situation I face.

A number of years ago, I heard a story about a crippled, single mother that underscores this attitude beautifully. She faithfully attended her church and had a passion to see it grow. She asked her pastor if she could start some children's Sunday school classes. He agreed, though privately he doubted she would be able to do much, given her handicap and the challenges of raising her own family alone. Little did this pastor know that he had unleashed a spiritual tigress!

Next, this woman decided the church really needed some buses to pick up children for Sunday school—and she wasn't going to just *wish* for it to happen. So, she herded her kids together, hobbled to the car with them, and drove off to a local commercial transportation company.

The company owner looked out the window as she drove up, seeing her painfully step out of her car and walk into his office. He listened as she plainly put her request to the dispatcher on duty. Of course, the dispatcher was stunned at the audacity of this mother. *Lend out our buses for Sunday school duty? No, there's no way we could do that, ma'am.*

The dispatcher's response was certainly logical. There would be insurance coverage to consider, overtime pay for drivers working on Sundays, and of course the gas, oil, and maintenance for the buses themselves. But instead of slinking out of the office defeated, the woman instead politely asked to speak to the boss.

Of course, the owner had been listening to the conversation. Though he felt compassion for the woman, he came in and firmly repeated all the reasons this just could not happen. Undeterred, this Sunday school dreamer passionately told him how the buses could have a huge, positive impact on the lives of children.

About then, a driver who had walked into the office and heard the exchange offered to volunteer his time to drive if the owner made a bus available. More conversation followed, but eventually—reluctantly—the owner found himself agreeing. *OK, one volunteer driver, one bus. No big deal,* he probably thought.

Neither this woman nor God was through yet, however. That volunteer driver's life was so touched by the experience of taking eager children to Sunday school that first weekend that he excitedly talked about the experience with other drivers. Within a few months, that woman's church was packed with kids learning about the Lord—and by then, half a dozen buses and drivers had been added to the church's Sunday school fleet!

One willing leader—despite her physical, economic, and social handicaps—had chosen to make every person and every place better because of Christ.

Pause right now and say with me, "I choose to make every person I meet and every place I go better because of Christ in me."

REFLECTIONS

I treasure this quotation from Dr. Charles Swindoll, the renowned pastor, writer, and President of Dallas Theological Seminary:

> The longer I live, the more I realize the impact of attitude on life. Attitude to me is more important than facts. It is more important than the past, than education, than wealth, than circumstances, than failures, than successes, than what others think or say or do. It is more important than appearance, giftedness, or skill. It will make or break a company...a church...a home. The remarkable thing is we have a choice everyday regarding the attitude we will embrace for that day. We cannot change the inevitable. The only thing we can do is play on the one string we have, and that is our attitude. I am convinced that life is 10% what happens to me and 90% how I react to it. And so it is with you. We are in charge of our attitudes.

I encourage you to reflect upon and respond to the following statements about attitude:

> *Lord, please forgive me for the poor attitude I have often displayed. Starting today, I choose:*
>   *To start acting and talking like God is in control.*
>   *To speak positively about others.*
>   *To let God control my thoughts and imagination.*

To be a thankful person.
To quickly forgive.
To be a problem-solver and not a whiner.
> *And to leave every person I meet and each place*
> *I go better because of Christ in me.*

Chapter Three

THE CARE OF THE LEADER

A N UNAVOIDABLE FACT of leadership is this: If you are going to be out in front of the troops, you also will become a prime target for the enemy. This is just as true for the Christian leader—*and our enemy is none other than Satan.*

When we come under such attacks, it is all too human to look for a hole to dive into. But God calls us to go *forward.* I am convinced that it is in times of crisis that we develop and prove the staying power of our most crucial values.

In the last job I had with the Air Force, I found myself under such attack. I had taken on a posting where morale was in the pits. In two years' time, much had turned around—morale was better, and most of the employees were happy with improvements made in the work environment...but not all were. The saying is true: You can hand some people gold bars, and they will still be unhappy!

In particular, some people had found common cause against me and my staff. One day, one of my leaders came into my office with a troubled look on his face and a homemade sign in his hand. The sign accused me and other leaders of favoritism and racism.

However, the real story here is the turmoil this smear campaign initially caused and how God turned the situation around. He brought a much-needed airing out and healing within the organization that left us more unified and stronger in purpose than ever.

Naturally, when I saw that sign, I was angry. I thought, *Satan, you are trying to come in and destroy everything good we've been able to build in this organization!* Then I prayed, asking the Lord for guidance in how I was to respond as a leader. The next day, I called an "all hands" meeting for our entire staff.

I had been inspired during my prayer time once again to turn to the acrostic tool. I felt led to write down the letters *CARE. This is a "care" issue,* the Lord impressed upon me, and within a half-hour, I had the whole message ready for the meeting.

You could have heard a pin drop as I fired up the overhead projector and began to share. I strongly felt God's presence with me and in that room. When I was done, the crowd gave that message a standing ovation; two staffers were so excited, they started making cards from the presentation's points and posting them everywhere.

The *CARE* principles—Communication, Accountability, Respect, and Expectations—were not new concepts, but the way God allowed me to share them that day was fresh and grabbed the hearts of my listeners. They also can be applied to situations within the secular world and church organizations alike.

"C" Stands for "Communication"

I listen to understand, not just to hear something to latch onto when I speak next. Honestly, most of us are not good listeners! Being a good listener takes time and focus. It is hard. I know that as a painful fact, and I know it from embarrassing personal experience.

Near the midpoint of my military career, I was the principal candidate for a key job. This was a plum assignment, as I would be interacting with most of the officers and enlisted personnel who served in my area of specialty. As you might guess, good listening skills were a must for this position.

The officer who would decide who would be selected for this assignment interviewed many people who had either worked with me or supervised me. The feedback was almost universally excellent, but there was one exception. A fellow worker told the officer I was not a good listener and that I tended to interrupt others before they could finish speaking.

When the selection officer asked me about it, at first I was defensive. But upon reflection, I had to admit the criticism was valid. I realized it was true. I did anticipate points being made, interrupting others in mid-sentence...and I not only did that in the workplace, but also at home with my family!

I was chagrined by the realization, and humbled. However, my honesty apparently made an impression; I was chosen for the job. I went into that posting with a new determination to become a better listener.

Oh, I still miss the mark at times, but I continue to this day to make it a priority in conversations to patiently listen before I respond.

It is, of course, very important *how* you listen. I've learned I need to listen with a desire to understand the other person's perspective. I try to put myself in their shoes, realizing that too often in the past I have just heard the words without understanding the attitudes, experiences, and expectations they represent. Without that perspective of the other, it is far too easy to jump to conclusions that are, at best, warped representations of the speaker's intent—if not just plain wrong.

By consciously taking steps to hear what is said from the other person's perspective, I have become more patient, understanding, and caring. When I put myself in the shoes of others, I am listening with not only my mind, but also my heart.

Listening is a tough but critical skill to learn. It also is just as important to exercise discipline in what we say. I do not repeat or listen to rumors but instead encourage myself and others to always seek the truth.

Easier said than done, you might say—and you'd be right. There is nothing like a rumor—that tasty morsel we hungrily digest and all-too-willingly share with others—to undermine the truth! Instead of learning what truly *is,* we are easily diverted to chasing half-truths (or no-truths) and speculation. That's why I slap an iron lid on that temptation. As mentioned earlier, here is a rule I try to live by:

> If I am not part of the solution, I will not listen to what others
> try to share with me about a situation or person.

Sadly, the rumor mill operates at full power in many organizations, and their leaders either try to ignore it or just toss up their hands in surrender, not knowing what else to do. I believe the right reaction for effective leaders is to roll up their sleeves and run toward this challenge. Simply put, if leaders want to bring the rumor mill to a halt, there's only one way: communicate, communicate, and then communicate some more!

The quicker you address the rumors, the better. And better yet, building a reputation of being open and honest with your staff and subordinates will help stop the rumor mill's grinding before it can gain momentum. Share as much information as you can, have question-and-answer sessions, put out memos, establish timely newsletters, and encourage your people to bring any rumors they hear to those Q&As.

In a nutshell, do everything you can to improve communication in the organization. Make it a top priority. As a leader, you may be convinced you understand a situation or challenge completely, but never assume others do. Find multiple, creative ways to get the word out and stop the rumor mill!

Another important aspect of a listening leader is never settling for one side of the story, no matter how convinced you are that what you have already heard is enough to make a decision. When you only listen to one side, you only get half the story. (Maybe you even get *less* than half!)

Let me give you an example from my own family. I have two wonderful grown children now. But I can remember numerous occasions when they were younger and one would tattle on the other. If you are a parent, this is familiar—and like I did, I bet you quickly learned to withhold your judgment until you had confronted the alleged wrongdoer. Not doing so—leaping to punishment based only on the tattling—leads to wrong actions you will later regret.

There are always two sides to every story, every dispute, and every allegation. I try to never make a decision in such cases without airing out both camps. That has not come easily for me, since it has been my nature to be decisive—to make a decision, determine the solution, and move on to the next issue.

Certainly my organizations have seldom bogged down in indecision, but that can be both good and bad. Sometimes, I admit, I have leapt to decisions before I had all the information—and then lamented my impatience. Unraveling a decision in order to make the correct move is always five times (or more) the headache for a leader and subordinates alike than taking the time to seek out and listen to both sides!

"A" STANDS FOR "ACCOUNTABILITY"

Accountability for the leader goes both ways. Of course, it is your responsibility, your calling, to watch for developing problems within your organization. But it also is your duty to offer solutions when you then bring up those challenges with an individual or your staff.

That lesson was driven home for me during my time under a rather unique leader. His manner, and often his language, were coarse. He was blunt and to the point. And because of those traits, I always knew where I stood with him. And I always found out where I stood with him quickly—and sometimes rather dramatically.

The time came when I was faced with a particularly thorny managerial problem, one where a solution just didn't seem clear. After several days of wrestling with this issue, I grew frustrated and came to see my boss. "I do not know what to do about this," I said after laying out the situation.

If I was expecting a pat on the back, soothing reassurance, or even for him to make the decision for me, I was rapidly shown the error of my ways. In fact, I was literally *shown the door!* That's right: He threw me out of his office, telling me in his rather folksy, earthy way that the next time I presented a problem to him, I had better be prepared to explain all the options I had considered and then give him my best recommendation.

I left his office a bit worse for wear, but as I calmed down and considered what had happened, I also was painfully wiser. This had been a very valuable lesson: Anyone can talk about problems, but it takes wisdom to offer solutions.

I regrouped, looked anew at the problem, went back to the general, laid out all the alternatives I had considered, and then gave him my recommendation. I still wasn't sure that recommendation was the best answer, but I knew at that point I had truly done all I could do. Then I braced myself for his response.

This time, let's just say I got to stay a bit longer in his office! Actually, I was amazed at the difference in the leader's response. He told me that I had done an excellent job addressing the problem and he would consider my recommendation.

I have a different personality and style of leadership than that general did, but I did adopt his philosophy on a leader's accountability in approaching challenges and seeking solutions. To this day, I encourage my people to never just bring a problem to me; I also want to hear their recommended solution.

Problems are like monkeys; they are messy, unruly, jump on our backs, tug at our hair and ears, and will drive us crazy if we let them. We just want to get them off us and out of the room. I never accept another's monkey unless they have at least tried to put a leash on the beast and can offer ideas on how to clean up its mess!

So, accountability is proactive. Leaders need to look for ways to create better workplace environments, and everyone should be involved in making the organization stronger and better. Leaders don't have all the answers; we need others' help and thoughtful perspectives. Often that means working hard to convince subordinates of your genuine desire for their input and how valuable it is to you.

Do that, and you will mobilize a body of people engaged in looking for ways to make their workplace, their mission, and their professional family better. This unity of purpose only comes when leaders and subordinates alike share ownership of their organizations and challenges.

Instill that sense of accountability, and a workplace culture grows where solutions cease to be "top down" but percolate from the ranks to leadership and back to the organization. Everyone owns a piece of the solutions and resulting successes, and all have the potential to be viewed by others—and perhaps more importantly, by themselves—as valuable contributors.

When there is a culture established that "this is our organization," things work better, problems get solved quicker, product and/or work quality improves, and complaints are reduced. And that attitude can and should go beyond the workplace. This is our country, our state, our city, our church, our family!

I can make a difference. When I help others, they can help me, too. That is the key belief that makes all the rest of this principle possible. It is just as true, though, that if I don't believe I can make a difference, I never will make a difference!

No one arrives at this conviction with the wave of a wand. That's where wise leadership comes in, deliberately and patiently building your staff members' sense of value as both individuals and contributors to the organization's mission and goals.

I have learned that life's biggest events started with little steps, and the same is true for the life of an organization. You certainly can think of events in your own life that echo this theme and realize that at the time you took those little steps, you had no idea where they would lead.

Building accountability within an organization starts with urging others to take those first steps—to share the seemingly insignificant idea, make the small change, or say the brief word of encouragement. These little things build, eventually having huge impacts on organizations.

We all can make a difference. We have something to contribute. We can help each other. We welcome other people's feedback to help us grow and do a better job.

"R" Stands for the Four "Rules of Respect"

1. I have learned to respect the difference in others.

This appreciation extends to not only the various personalities I've encountered over the years, but to others' perspectives and the giftings they bring to the table.

Frankly, extremely innovative people used to irritate me. They seemed full of ideas, but to me these dreamers never seemed to accomplish much. They were in love with concepts but not so much with the hard work needed to turn them into reality. At least, that was my assessment.

My style and personality are very much practically oriented. I want to see ideas come to fruition. That is what makes them worthwhile to me. I've come to appreciate both the dreamers and the doers, though. In my career, I've seen where God brought those innovative dreamers into my life as either my deputies or superiors. The Lord was balancing the leadership equation! My irritation with these innovators has melted away with this realization: I *needed* their ideas to be fully effective as a leader, and as the practical, results-oriented part of this formula, it was my job to help the dreamers implement their ideas.

These imaginative commanders and staffers have brought freshness to my leadership performance. Where such differences in approach and abilities used to frustrate me, I can honestly say today that I greatly appreciate those differences. I love to have diverse perspectives available on my leadership team. I value the blessing of being able to look at things differently through those innovative eyes.

When you think about it, reaching out for people who have strengths in areas we lack is very human. I often marvel how people marry someone who is their opposite. That can work well for both partners if they realize those perspectives and abilities should complement rather than conflict with each other. Balance is the goal, or it should be. Without balance, however, marriages crumble and leadership teams fragment and become ineffective.

I have mentioned that seeking out those who have strengths we do not is a human trait. So is what I like to call the *bias trap*—the tendency to favor and promote people who think and lead like we do.

Face it: The best future leader may not be your clone! Different leadership styles are a good thing, not something to be politely tolerated. I would hate seeing a world filled only with leaders who thought, spoke, and acted like me!

So, where do we as leaders fit into all this? We help our people use their differences in a balanced, life-giving way. I can bring a perspective to them that will empower and make them more effective, and they can do the same for me. The Bible agrees: "As iron sharpens iron, so one man sharpens another" (Prov. 27:17, NIV).

Look beyond the sparks that can fly when differing perspectives and temperaments collide. Realize that these different others are the ones who make us sharper! We need to love the diversity of God's creation…the forests and mountains, the valleys and deserts, plant and animal life, the land or the sea, and people.

> He has made everything beautiful in its time. He has also set eternity in the hearts of men; yet they cannot fathom what God has done from beginning to end.
> —ECCLESIASTES 3:11, NIV

Yes! Diversity is beautiful. Diversity is good.

2. I try not to attribute motives to what others say and do; only God can do that.

I touched on this point earlier, but it bears repeating: Usually we don't become angry with what others say and do; we become angry about the apparent reason they did or said what they did. In other words, we attribute motives to people's words and actions.

Certainly, there are times when we are correct in our speculations on others' motives—but admit it: usually we are not. Most often we don't truly know the motives of others until we ask them. So, never assume anything; ask the questions!

3. I have perceptions, and so do others, but I realize perceptions are personal and not absolute.

If you are making a change in your organization of one hundred people, you will have at least one hundred opinions about the change.

Perceptions are birthed in a cauldron boiling with many ingredients. This organizational recipe contains dollops of differences in the way individuals are raised; a dash consisting of what position with a company or church a person holds; a pinch of attitude an individual had when he or she came to work that morning; even an array of seasonings—what a person ate for breakfast, the state of their health, whether they had a fight with a spouse or child, and many other random factors that life thrusts upon us all.

As true as all those things are, leaders cannot afford to ignore the myriad perceptions and reactions they will inevitably encounter. I suggest the best way to deal with perceptions is the same way we address the rumor mill: confront them and air them out.

Remember that someone's stand on an issue often relies heavily on where they sit within the organization. Perspective is colored by the individual's position and past experiences. That said, the underlying principle here is that perceptions are a powerful force in any organization. People within it, leaders and subordinates alike, need to realize that their perceptions can often be wrong.

4. No task, position, or person is more valuable than another.

In one of my military positions, I had an assigned driver. He was the epitome of the team player who did his job with diligence and humility, despite having what some might perceive as a humble position in life.

I did a lot of traveling in order to keep an eye on subordinate organizations, and there also were monthly trips to report to my own superiors. In other words, I kept my driver busy, taking me to and from the airport, and his professional demeanor, mixed with his care for my needs, meant a lot to me.

My driver was always on time, which would have been enough. But he always made it a point to ask about my family, genuinely and personally being concerned with our welfare. In turn, I made it a point to tell him how much I appreciated his attitude. That quiet excellence in his work and demeanor impressed me as much as any other person who had worked for me.

There are many such people in military operations, businesses, and churches alike for whom their work or calling is sufficient reward. They don't win the accolades or envy of others who may see their positions as lackluster, yet these seemingly anonymous laborers can exercise influence beyond their stations through their attitudes.

Another wonderful employee I worked with was a secretary. I am convinced she was just as important to the success of my organization as many of my subordinate leaders. It was common for me to hear that she was one of the most helpful people on my staff.

Praise usually flows to the top. But for any organization, the white-collar or command positions are no more important to success than blue-collar or supportive positions. In football, the quarterbacks may get the headlines, but without the nameless linemen who protect him, the hero would be on his back most of the time, waiting for his head to stop spinning.

By not recognizing this truth and by going out of our way to throw kudos only to those who fill the "important" roles, we send a wrong, even demoralizing signal to the so-called rank-and-file folks who make any organization's goals and dreams reality. Here's what the Bible has to say about that:

> In fact, some parts of the body that seem weakest and least important are actually the most necessary. And the parts we regard as less honorable are those we clothe with the greatest care. So we carefully protect those parts that should not be seen, while the more honorable parts do not require this special care. So God has put the body together such that extra honor and care are given to those parts that have less dignity. This makes for harmony among the members, so that all the members care for each other. If one part suffers, all the parts suffer with it, and if one part is honored, all the parts are glad.
> —1 CORINTHIANS 12:22–26, NLT

"E" Stands for the Four "Expectation Principles"

1. I come here to work hard and enjoy my fellow workers.

Expectations are powerful forces in our lives. They motivate us or drag us down. An effective leader works hard and expects others to do the same. You can crack the whip and growl out orders, but balancing a positive work ethic with a caring workplace environment is the way to build a happy, mutually supportive and productive organizational family.

Ignore the social needs of your people, and you will miss out on a powerful motivator—that of appreciating each person not only as a worker but as a treasured member of your corporate or church family!

I always look for ways to get people to interact: picnics, discussion groups, projects, and recreational activities. This is an investment of your leadership time, though not directly related to the organization's goals that will pay big dividends. Such interaction, in the workplace and outside of it, builds good relationships based on more than just specific assignments and duties.

I want to look forward to coming to work, and I look for ways to spark that same attitude in my staff and subordinates. And that desire is not just motivated by the organizational bottom line but because, as a Christian leader, I care about the quality of life my people enjoy away from work, too.

When a person feels that their ideas will be welcomed and fairly considered—and that they won't be hammered for honest mistakes—they are far more likely to embrace interaction with other team members and relish hard work.

2. I look at problems as opportunities to make my organization even better.

How do you view problems? Count on it—your people will be inclined to approach challenges and difficulties the same way you do. If your reaction is impatience, frustration, or even hostility when someone tells you about a problem, no one will bring things to your attention that need to be fixed. Instead, problems that may have been nipped in the bud will grow into catastrophes that may exact a steep price in angst and energy to solve.

I have never "killed the messenger," as the saying goes, but I used to *hate* problems. In fact, it was my tendency to run away from them if I could. Years ago, God rebuked me for that attitude. His message to me was, "Find a way to run toward, not away, from problems."

Now I am resolute in seeing problems as opportunities, as chances to make myself better, for my team members to grow, and, ultimately, to make the organization's environment stronger through the experience of confronting and resolving problems head on. Naturally, I still don't leap for joy when a particularly nasty challenge rears up, but I can honestly say I now calmly find ways to run toward them.

Yes, problems—and how you choose to handle them—not only reveal character strengths or flaws a leader may have, but they can also lead to corrective measures that will make us and our organizations stronger.

3. If I expect nothing to change, I will probably get what I expect.

I have often heard others comment, "Nothing will ever change around here." What they say is probably true for them. Even when things do change, people with negative expectations don't recognize or are not pleased with the changes. Such attitudes can be pivotal in our lives, since our expectations shape how we approach our jobs, our families, our finances, our churches, and even our God!

Charles Spurgeon, the nineteenth-century English preacher, once said, "You might not always get what you want, but you always get what you expect." In large measure, I believe this is true. Negative attitudes have a way of becoming self-fulfilling prophecies; if you expect setbacks, you give little ground for good things to happen in life or in the workplace.

Negative expectations are like throwing dirt into a mountain stream and then complaining about how bad the water tastes!

So, what role does the leader play in this equation? Leaders should be the most positive people in their workplace, church, or other organization.

4. If I am unhappy here, I will probably be unhappy somewhere else; the same "me" goes to the new place.

Change, no matter the external factors that may bring its need to light, always starts on the *inside* of a person. We all know people who wish it was the weekend, next week, next month, or next year, or those who just wish they were someplace else! These are the folks who seldom enjoy the moment but instead believe that if only their circumstances were different, life would be better.

Of course, there are times when it is true that a change does improve a person's quality of life. Still, circumstances—where we work or teach or pastor, or to whom or with we do those things—are not the most important factors in whether we are happy or not. As I wrote earlier, it is *attitude* that has, by far, the biggest impact on our lives. A good attitude trumps our abilities or our circumstances; indeed, a healthy attitude can be the catalyst for bolstering our abilities and transforming circumstances!

I have discovered that if I leave a position, a church, or a relationship with a bad attitude, then the reason for moving on often is wrong. Our new circumstances may be changed, but without the right attitude, we almost always will end up worse than those we left.

I once had to turn down a subordinate's request for a transfer from one position to another. I refused because his attitude was so negative that he had become a source of constant irritation within my organization. I frankly told him I could not justify making him another organization's problem. However, I promised him that if his attitude improved, I would consider his request again and that with his experience, other units probably would fight to get him.

I hoped this incentive, along with suggestions I offered on ways to turn things around, would help him. Unfortunately, he rejected the overtures, continued to wallow in the pit he had dug for himself, and eventually resigned.

REFLECTIONS

If you want to be a godly leader and help others to become the same, it boils down to modeling and teaching *communication, accountability, respect,* and *expectations.* Practice and share those principles, and you and the organizations you lead will be better.

My prayer for you and myself is that we will run our race well, that we will lead with care, and that we will encourage others to do the same by word and example!

Chapter Four

THE DILIGENCE OF THE LEADER

OST OF US reach a point in our lives where we mentally just
stop, look around at where life has taken us, and how we've
gotten there—*and marvel.*

That time came for me a little over halfway through my Air Force
career. I remember that "conversation" with God as I reviewed scenes
and relived memories of what had happened both professionally and
personally. It was a humbling experience that had me shaking my
head with amazement and gratitude.

At that point in time, my career had been going very well. I had
been honored with selection by a number of prestigious schools and
had twice been promoted ahead of my peers. "God, why me?" I asked.
"There are many others who are more deserving and certainly more
talented."

God gave me an intriguing answer through what I like to call a
heart thought. It went like this: "I have blessed you because you have
been diligent."

Some folks would be content with that, believing a quick look at the
dictionary would show them that *hard work* equates to *diligence*. But I
wanted to know what God meant by this, so I embarked on an intense
scriptural word study. What I found was that the Lord's idea of diligence was far more than just working hard.

Between the pages of my Bible, I discovered a powerful formula
that connected our diligence with God's power. The number of areas
where God specifically commanded diligence particularly challenged
me. Further, I noted that there were incredible rewards for diligence.

Diligence: A Definition

Webster's Dictionary defines diligence as "steady, earnest, energetic effort." Scripture paints a picture of the word that is far more expansive. I've come to believe that God's standard of diligence is that whatever I do, I do it *promptly, earnestly, carefully, energetically, and with humility.*

- Doing something *promptly* means not waiting to be asked to do something, beginning a task as soon as you can, and completing it as soon as possible.

- Doing something *earnestly* means choosing to do a task with the right attitude, hanging in there even when the task is very difficult, and putting your heart into whatever you do.

- Doing something *carefully* means doing a quality job, giving your best effort to whatever you do, and paying attention to even the smallest of details.

- Doing something *energetically* means working very hard, staying with the task until it is done, and being a good example to others.

- Doing something with *humility* means not being motivated by ideas of reward but doing whatever you do to the glory of God and serving out of a love for Jesus Christ.

This definition of *diligence*—one I believe is God-inspired—certainly is more complex and layered in meaning than *Webster's.* However, this definition and its touchstones of acting promptly, earnestly, carefully, energetically, and with humility has helped me better understand what God asks of leaders—you and me—in His kingdom. It is my prayer that the Holy Spirit will plant those attributes in us all!

A Divine Equation

Ultimately, our diligence belongs to God. He should be in our minds and hearts as the overarching recipient of our prompt, earnest, careful, and energetic efforts, regardless of the task or challenge. Only by recognizing Him, the rightful originator and owner of our dedicated work, can we sustain the final, critical element of diligence: humility.

The Bible makes it clear that committing our diligence to God is part of the divine equation for blessings and success for an inspired leader:

> Whatever your hand finds to do, do it with all your might, for in the grave, where you are going, there is neither working nor planning nor knowledge nor wisdom.
> —ECCLESIASTES 9:10, NIV

> So whether you eat or drink or whatever you do, do it all for the glory of God.
> —1 CORINTHIANS 10:31, NIV

> And whatever you do, whether in word or deed, do it all in the name of the Lord Jesus, giving thanks to God the Father through him.
> —COLOSSIANS 3:17, NIV

So, we start by dedicating our talents, gifts, and experiences to God, and then we use what we have been given to the best of our ability. That is the beginning of godly diligence. And when we are diligent in this way, God honors the commitment and attitude by adding a wonderful ingredient: His supernatural power!

His power with our diligence brings results beyond what we could have ever achieved on our own. Here's a formula for success as a leader that will never fail:

My Diligence + God's Power = Supernatural Results

Have you noticed a startling truth here? *What God does through me does not depend on my talents, abilities, or gifts.* What the Lord can accomplish through us depends on the degree we dedicate what we have to Him, and then doing our best. God does not play favorites, only working through the so-called "superstars" of faith we see on Christian television or behind the pulpits of megachurches. He works through those who are willing and determined to serve Him with whatever they have.

Then the miracles come when God adds His supernatural power to our diligence!

God's Diligence "Pressure Cooker"

Say the words *pressure cooker,* and often the first reaction is negative. No one likes the idea until they realize how valuable and beneficial this time-honored cooking device can be. For example, chefs will brag that the pressure cooker retains more of the vitamins and minerals in food; cooks food up to 70 percent faster than mere boiling or steaming; uses less energy in the long run; and usually is cleaner (with that lid locked on, there are no spatters or spills).

Pressure cooker works just as well as a metaphor for how God prepares His leaders! Consider this scripture:

> Be assured and understand that the trial and proving of your
> faith bring out endurance and steadfastness and patience.
> —James 1:3, amp

Endurance, steadfastness, and patience are traits produced by godly diligence. They are words that express diligence. Unfortunately, most of us are not naturally diligent, especially when those characteristics are the standards by which we are measured. So, diligence is largely a learned quality.

Thankfully, God knows each of us intimately, and He lovingly crafts situations and circumstances in which our diligence can grow. Like the potter working a lump of clay, He pulls, stretches, pushes, and pressures us as leaders in ways we would have never chosen on our own. That is what I mean by being in God's pressure cooker.

Our Lord will not relent until we develop the diligence we so desperately need. That is something I have come to trust, even (painfully) crave as a leader. I gulp a bit first, perhaps, but I welcome pressure, trials, and testing as "tough love" friends teaching me diligence!

Of course, I wish there was another way, but God has chosen to use pressure and trials to produce the fruit of diligence in us.

AREAS WHERE GOD'S WORD COMMANDS DILIGENCE

The Bible consistently proclaims God's expectations for and commands to exercise diligence. As I studied this principle, I was amazed how frequently that theme is underscored within the Lord's equation for effective leadership.

Here is just a smattering of the many examples I found.

Teaching the Scriptures to your children.

> "You shall teach them diligently to your children, and shall talk of them when you sit in your house, when you walk by the way, when you lie down, and when you rise up."
>
> —DEUTERONOMY 6:7

Living life according to God's principles.

> "You shall diligently keep the commandments of the LORD your God, His testimonies, and His statutes which He has commanded you."
>
> —DEUTERONOMY 6:17

Keeping Jesus on the "throne" of your life.

> Keep your heart with all diligence, for out of it spring the issues of life.
>
> —PROVERBS 4:23

Being a good steward of the job, responsibilities, and possessions God has given you.

> Be diligent to know the state of your flocks, and attend to your herds; for riches are not forever, nor does a crown endure to all generations.
>
> —PROVERBS 27:23–24

Quickly resolving quarrels and issues with others.

> "Then as you go with your accuser before a magistrate, on the way make a diligent effort to settle and be quit (free) of him, lest he drag you to the judge, and the judge turn you over to the officer, and the officer put you in prison."
>
> —Luke 12:58, amp

Working hard at being a good leader.

> We have different gifts, according to the grace given us. If a man's gift is...leadership, let him govern diligently.
>
> —Romans 12:6, 8, niv

Giving sacrificially.

> But as you abound in everything—in faith, in speech, in knowledge, in all diligence, and in your love for us—see that you abound in this grace [sacrificial giving] also.
>
> —2 Corinthians 8:7

Visiting and communicating with other leaders.

> Be diligent to come to me quickly.
>
> —2 Timothy 4:9

Serving and loving others.

> God is not unjust; he will not forget your work and the love you have shown him as you have helped his people and continue to help them. We want each of you to show this same diligence to the very end, in order to make your hope sure.
>
> —Hebrews 6:10–11, niv

Developing character qualities.

> But also for this very reason, giving all diligence, add to your faith virtue, to virtue knowledge, to knowledge self-control, to self-control perseverance, to perseverance godliness, to godliness brotherly kindness, and to brotherly kindness love. For if

these things are yours and abound, you will be neither barren nor unfruitful in the knowledge of our Lord Jesus Christ.

—2 PETER 1:5–8

Doing nothing that will reflect poorly on your walk as a believer in Jesus Christ.

Therefore, brethren, be even more diligent to make your call and election sure, for if you do these things you will never stumble.

—2 PETER 1:10

THE REWARDS OF DILIGENCE

We have discussed in some detail what God expects of us in terms of diligence. But now let's talk about the rewards the Lord promises for leaders who dedicate themselves to that hard-working, trusting, and selfless perspective. The Bible makes many promises in this regard.

Abundant provision from your work.

Lazy hands make a man poor, but diligent hands bring wealth.

—PROVERBS 10:4, NIV

What you have goes a long way.

Lazy people don't even cook the game they catch, but the diligent make use of everything they find.

—PROVERBS 12:27, NLT

Blessing from doing the right things.

He who diligently seeks good seeks [God's] favor, but he who searches after evil, it shall come upon him.

—PROVERBS 11:27, AMP

It is well with your soul.

The soul of a lazy man desires, and has nothing; but the soul of the diligent shall be made rich.

—PROVERBS 13:4

Plans prosper.

The plans of the diligent lead surely to plenty, but those of everyone who is hasty, surely to poverty.

—PROVERBS 21:5

Recognition and advancement.

Do you see a man diligent and skillful in his business? He will stand before kings; he will not stand before obscure men.

—PROVERBS 22:29, AMP

Answered prayers.

But without faith it is impossible to please Him, for he who comes to God must believe that He is, and that He is a rewarder of those who diligently seek Him.

—HEBREWS 11:6

REFLECTIONS

In what areas are you not diligent?

- Pause right now and ask God to show you these areas.

- Ask God's forgiveness.

- Commit to give God your diligence in any area where He convicts you.

- Have you complained that you are not talented or gifted?

- Repent for any complaining you have done concerning the talent, abilities, and gifts God gave you.

- Realize that talent, abilities, and giftedness are not the issues.

- See that the "great equalizer" is the diligence you give to God.

- Understand that God's power added to your diligence brings supernatural results.

As a leader, pray the following prayer of commitment:

Lord, I commit to do whatever I do promptly. I won't wait to be asked; I won't procrastinate on starting tasks; and I will complete the task as soon as possible. Whatever I do, I will do it earnestly and with the right attitude. I will hang in there when the going gets tough and put my heart into whatever I do.

Whatever I do, I will do it carefully, giving it my very best and paying attention to detail. Whatever I do, I will do it energetically, working hard, staying with a task until it is done, and trying my best to be a good example to others. Finally, whatever I do, I will do it humbly, not seeking credit or a reward, but doing it because I love Jesus Christ.

Amen.

Chapter Five

THE COURAGE OF THE LEADER

I F I TELL you that the prime character requirement of a leader is courage, you might cock your head, look at me with polite (well, I hope) amusement, and mutter to yourself, *Well, yes. And cookies go well with cold milk, too.*

Of course courage is elemental to an effective leader's personality, and in particular a godly leader. But I'm talking about something beyond the stereotypical image many of us see when we hear the word *courage*—a John Wayne sort of character who is first into the fray, out in front of his troops, under fire, and encouraging troops to engage the enemy.

That is certainly a kind of courage. But a Christian leader's courage runs much deeper and broader than that; it must be a multifaceted, overarching character trait, an attitude and way of living that is way beyond describing in one chapter of this book! Still, the Lord has given me some thoughts on the subject, and I pray they will spark your own internal and spiritual exploration of courage as it applies to life, work, and ministry.

COURAGE: A DEFINITION

Beyond the fortitude it takes to risk your life for others, I believe courage is the moral, mental, and physical strength to face, withstand, and persevere in the face of danger, fear, or difficulty. It could mean firmly, uncompromisingly saying no to a bad choice. It requires more than just physical strength. And it also enlists your mind, your heart, and your convictions.

So, courage can mean facing a dangerous situation or facing your fears. Whatever form your call for courage takes, it is certain that the battlegrounds where it will be tested vary for each of us.

That said, I am convinced there are seven specific arenas where those aspiring to be godly leaders will be tested.

SEVEN ASPECTS OF COURAGE

The first testing ground for leadership courage? *Admitting you have a need or a problem to begin with.*

This is one of many, and perhaps the most difficult of challenges for many leaders! After all, by definition, leaders are supposed to be strong. These are the folks expected to have all the answers, or least know where to get them. As a leader, conventional wisdom maintains you cannot afford to reveal any holes in your armor.

I am not saying leadership means being the opposite of that stereotype. Godly, effective leaders are neither totally self-sufficient lone wolves, nor are they supposed to be continually sharing all their fears, doubts, and weaknesses with those they lead. However, they do need to bring those needs and problems to God by means of honest and vulnerable petitions.

They also need to share these needs or problems with trusted subordinates and peers. I believe Jesus demonstrated this during a time of agonizing struggle with His own humanity:

> Then Jesus came with them to a place called Gethsemane, and said to the disciples, "Sit here while I go and pray over there." And He took with Him Peter and the two sons of Zebedee, and He began to be sorrowful and deeply distressed. Then He said to them, "My soul is exceedingly sorrowful, even to death. Stay here and watch with Me."
>
> He went a little farther and fell on His face, and prayed, saying, "O My Father, if it is possible, let this cup pass from Me; nevertheless, not as I will, but as You will."
>
> Then He came to the disciples and found them sleeping, and said to Peter, "What! Could you not watch with Me one hour? Watch and pray, lest you enter into temptation. The spirit indeed is willing, but the flesh is weak."
>
> Again, a second time, He went away and prayed, saying, "O My Father, if this cup cannot pass away from Me unless I

drink it, Your will be done." And He came and found them asleep again, for their eyes were heavy.

—MATTHEW 26:36–43

This soul-rending picture of Christ's passage through His final valley of decision leading to Mount Calvary always touches me deeply. Here is a Jesus who was transparent, honest, and vulnerable—not only with His Father but also with His closest disciples, His friends.

The Son of God showed us that sharing a need with a trusted subordinate is not a sign of weakness; rather, it is a model of a different kind of strength. Showing such trust and openness gives those under your authority permission to be honest with you, too. Yes, everyone has needs and faces problems.

Women seem to have this whole sharing thing down pat. Men seem to have a more difficult time opening up, but finding that ability is crucial to becoming the kind of leader God wants. Indeed, I have found great strength, comfort, and a reservoir of help is opened to me when I am honest about my needs and problems.

I will go even further than that. I am convinced that many of our needs will never be met and our problems will go unresolved *without* the prayerful assistance of others. That is how God has made us, after all: to need the love and help of others. Consider these insights from the Bible:

> But God made our bodies with many parts, and he has put each part just where he wants it. What a strange thing a body would be if it had only one part! Yes, there are many parts, but only one body. The eye can never say to the hand, "I don't need you." The head can't say to the feet, "I don't need you."
>
> In fact, some of the parts that seem weakest and least important are really the most necessary. And the parts we regard as less honorable are those we clothe with the greatest care. So we carefully protect from the eyes of others those parts that should not be seen, while other parts do not require this special care.
>
> So God has put the body together in such a way that extra honor and care are given to those parts that have less dignity. This makes for harmony among the members, so that all

the members care for each other equally. If one part suffers, all the parts suffer with it, and if one part is honored, all the parts are glad.

—1 CORINTHIANS 12:18–26, NLT

It takes real courage to admit that you have a need or problem, and we become stronger as we do that. I have learned that in the workplace, to be sure; but perhaps my best teacher for acquiring this kind of courage has been my dear wife, Debbe.

For many years, Debbe and I have made it a point to participate in small home groups at the various churches where we have pastored or attended. Typically, those get-togethers wrap up with prayer requests. I've always been fine with praying *for* someone, but sharing my own needs has been very hard for me. Not so with Debbe, and her example of openness has spurred me on to becoming more transparent with my own challenges in such group settings.

My wife has been, and will always be, a source of encouragement and pillar of strength for me. I pray you, too, will be blessed with such a spouse!

Number two on my list for tests of courage is *discovering the ability to speak up for the underdog.*

God expects leaders to stand up for those unable to stand up for themselves! God watches how we help the broken, the discouraged, the hurting, and the rejected. Bottom line: *Leaders take care of people.* It is not just about accomplishing our goals and dreams; our mission includes the team we lead, and it cannot be accomplished without those role players.

You will never, ever have a team made up of perfect members. Some leaders never seem to realize that and spend a lot of time and fruitless energy tweaking their organizational charts. But instead of first looking to trade away some of the members of your team like so many baseball cards, maybe they just need someone to believe in them and speak up for them! And that someone could be *you.*

The Bible recounts how King David not only came to that conclusion, but also was proactive about moving forward from that realization. Instead of getting rid of the family and court and military officials left over from King Saul's regime, he reached out to them. He spoke up for the underdogs.

He took a chance—a big one—that his courageous compassion would be rewarded with loyal service. Here is one example:

> Now David said, "Is there still anyone who is left of the house of Saul, that I may show him kindness for Jonathan's sake?"
>
> And there was a servant of the house of Saul whose name was Ziba. So when they had called him to David, the king said to him, "Are you Ziba?"
>
> He said, "At your service!"
>
> Then the king said, "Is there not still someone of the house of Saul, to whom I may show the kindness of God?"
>
> And Ziba said to the king, "There is still the son of Jonathan who is lame in his feet."
>
> So the king said to him, "Where is he?"
>
> And Ziba said to the king, "Indeed he is in the house of Machir the son of Ammiel, in Lo Debar."
>
> Then King David sent and brought him out of the house of Machir the son of Ammiel, from Lo Debar.
>
> Now when Mephibosheth the son of Jonathan, the son of Saul, had come to David, he fell on his face and prostrated himself. Then David said, "Mephibosheth?"
>
> And he answered, "Here is your servant!"
>
> So David said to him, "Do not fear, for I will surely show you kindness for Jonathan your father's sake, and will restore to you all the land of Saul your grandfather; and you shall eat at my table continually."
>
> —2 SAMUEL 9:1–7

It was this sort of compassion I witnessed some years ago from an Air Force captain and his wife who attended church with Debbe and me. This couple, despite having their own small children to care for, invited a homeless woman and her young son to live with them. In so many ways, at least by the world's standards, this was quite a risky decision.

After all, this scary looking street woman with her missing front teeth and dirty, ragged clothing had just shown up at church. Her language was often coarse; she was on first—and perhaps second or even third—impression an unattractive person, both in appearance and temperament. I even recall saying to myself when this couple made their invitation, "Oh! Guys, do you know what you are doing?"

But God knew all this woman needed was a few months respite from the streets and someone who would take a chance on her and her boy. This couple took that risk and brought her into their home. They were positive with her, supportive emotionally, and helped her clean up her appearance and language. Their example encouraged others to pitch in, too, including some who helped her get a key job interview.

Soon, she had landed a job and was shortly thereafter promoted. She and her son moved out and got their own apartment. It was a complete transformation for this formerly homeless, hopeless mother and her boy.

What was the special ingredient that changed her life? I believe it was someone believing in and, by their actions, speaking up for her. Leaders have the privilege and responsibility to do that for others!

Number three on my courage "hit parade" is *being able to say, "That is not right."*

Sadly, this is a quality that is growing increasingly rare. It is so much more politically savvy to verbally skirt around tough issues or just stay quiet. It takes courage, though, to speak up when you see something happening that you know is not right—even when many others, maybe even all of your peers, enthusiastically support that wrong or allow it to happen without a peep of protest.

The issue could be as simple as deciding not to take an unethical shortcut, or standing firm on principles when they are challenged or assailed. Here is how the Apostle Paul modeled such fortitude in spirit and action:

> But when Peter came to Antioch, I had to oppose him publicly, speaking strongly against what he was doing, for it was very wrong. When he first arrived, he ate with the Gentile Christians, who don't bother with circumcision. But afterward, when some Jewish friends of James came, Peter wouldn't eat with the Gentiles anymore because he was afraid of what these legalists would say. Then the other Jewish Christians followed Peter's hypocrisy, and even Barnabas was influenced to join them in their hypocrisy.
>
> When I saw that they were not following the truth of the

Good News, I said to Peter in front of all the others, "Since you, a Jew by birth, have discarded the Jewish laws and are living like a Gentile, why are you trying to make these Gentiles obey the Jewish laws you abandoned?"

—Galatians 2:11–14, NLT

While Peter was visiting the Gentile church in Antioch, he lovingly interacted with them, even though this was new territory for Jewish Christians. He ate what they ate, probably not strictly kosher fare, and he didn't try to convince the men to submit to circumcision, either.

But when a group of less liberated Jewish Christians arrived from Jerusalem, believers who still held to their traditional dietary rituals, Peter started behaving differently. Peter was afraid of the criticism he might receive from the visitors and became a hypocrite, but Paul didn't let him get by with it. Paul called Peter on it publicly, and it took great courage for this newcomer to the apostolic ranks to confront the one leader Jesus Himself has called the "rock" of the fledgling faith.

It took guts for Paul to call the revered "Big Fisherman" to account; it also takes great courage for every leader today to stand up and say, "That is not right."

One such modern-day hero is Dr. James Dobson of Focus on the Family. He has stood up for Christian family values for many years and paid the price in being the target of great personal ridicule from secular leaders and the press. I admire his courage and leadership to say, "That is wrong and this is right."

Number four on my list of courageous traits is *being able to say, "I was wrong."*

I have met very few people in the so-called rank-and-file who find it easy to say these words, and it seems especially difficult for a leader to make such a confession! After all, leaders are held to a higher standard, and however unfair that is in some respects, they are expected to be right all the time.

Yes, that is what people expect of their leaders, but I'm a prime example that this is just not so.

Early in our marriage, I was inwardly very judgmental of the more traditional, non-charismatic denominational faith of my wife Debbe's parents. They, in turn, were somewhat uncomfortable with the more emotional, demonstrative nature of our Pentecostal worship.

While I never said anything to them about how I felt, my attitude nonetheless put up barriers between us. Secret prejudices can do that; I may not have told them I felt their faith expression was inferior to my own, but that attitude came out in other ways.

About six years into our marriage, the Lord convicted me; actually, the guilt I felt was more like torment. I felt extremely ashamed, even compelled to call Debbe's folks, confess, and ask their forgiveness!

One problem: This was before the easy communication of cell phones, and my in-laws were on vacation. Desperate as I was to make things right, I didn't know how to reach my mother- and father-in-law. So, I prayed: "Lord, You've put this on my heart. Please help me find a way to contact them."

Literally, within sixty seconds after that prayer, our phone rang. On the other end of the line were my in-laws. Debbe was in the shower, so I had been the one to pick up the phone, and I almost gasped when I heard their voices. But after the initial shock, I swallowed once or twice and asked their forgiveness for my judgmental attitude.

Their response was incredibly gracious. While they insisted they had not felt judgment from me, I knew that my attitude nonetheless had been dishonoring to both God and them and that it had affected our relationship in unseen ways. My mother- and father-in-law were deeply touched by my words, quickly granted the forgiveness I sought, and from then on were very open about their faith with us and often called asking for our prayers.

Even the Apostle Paul had to admit he was wrong—and to do so to the very enemies who were seeking his life for preaching the Gospel: the chief priests and the religious leaders of Jerusalem's Sanhedrin. In a hearing before the Roman military commander, though he was being falsely accused and physically mistreated, this apostle had the courage to repent of his own misbehavior.

Here is an account of that incident from the Bible:

> Paul looked straight at the Sanhedrin and said, "My brothers, I have fulfilled my duty to God in all good conscience to this day." At this the high priest Ananias ordered those standing near Paul to strike him on the mouth. Then Paul said to him, "God will strike you, you whitewashed wall! You sit there to

judge me according to the law, yet you yourself violate the law by commanding that I be struck!"

Those who were standing near Paul said, "You dare to insult God's high priest?"

Paul replied, "Brothers, I did not realize that he was the high priest; for it is written: 'Do not speak evil about the ruler of your people.'"

—Acts 23:1–5, NIV

Paul knew that true integrity shines through when our commitment to truth and principle is both internally and externally applied. He knew that while it is easy for leaders to deal with situations from the firm footing of being in the right, it can be a tough test, indeed, when we find ourselves in the wrong.

Truth is, few leaders in our world today are humble enough to admit they have taken a stand or made a decision in error.

I have learned three steps to take when I have found myself in the wrong.

First, *admit the wrong publicly.* Painful, yes; humiliating, perhaps. But silent or muted confession does little good to those who have been impacted by wrong actions, words, or decisions. We need to be public in dealing with errors.

Second, *correct errors, words, or actions quickly.* The longer we wait, the worse the situation can become.

Finally, be sure to humbly say the words, *"I was wrong."* An arrogant non-apology or confession tells everyone that you are an arrogant leader. So, the admission needs to use those inescapable, uncompromising, and from-the-heart words: *"I was wrong."*

Number five on my courage list? *Having the guts to be different from the crowd.*

To be a leader—the kind worthy of God's blessings and your fellows' respect—is to be able to make the difficult decisions. The right decision may not be the popular decision; indeed, it may be downright unpopular.

Think about it: How many of our politicians today seem to swap their "firm convictions" on the issues every time the winds of popular opinion cause the latest poll to flop to one side or the other? Decisions made on that basis, riding the emotions of the masses, are easy to make. But what of the long-term consequences? Often, the right decision is met with anger and disdain, only to be proven correct as events unfold.

Making the right decision, then gritting your teeth and weathering the storm of protests, takes guts. Scripture gives us many examples of such courage, like the one involving the Old Testament heroes Joshua and Caleb. They stood firm against public opinion, even at the risk of their lives:

> That night all the people of the community raised their voices and wept aloud. All the Israelites grumbled against Moses and Aaron, and the whole assembly said to them, "If only we had died in Egypt! Or in this desert! Why is the Lord bringing us to this land only to let us fall by the sword? Our wives and children will be taken as plunder. Wouldn't it be better for us to go back to Egypt?" And they said to each other, "We should choose a leader and go back to Egypt."
>
> Then Moses and Aaron fell face down in front of the whole Israelite assembly gathered there. Joshua son of Nun and Caleb son of Jephunneh, who were among those who had explored the land, tore their clothes and said to the entire Israelite assembly, "The land we passed through and explored is exceedingly good. If the Lord is pleased with us, he will lead us into that land, a land flowing with milk and honey, and will give it to us. Only do not rebel against the Lord. And do not be afraid of the people of the land, because we will swallow them up. Their protection is gone, but the Lord is with us. Do not be afraid of them."
>
> But the whole assembly talked about stoning them.
>
> —NUMBERS 14:1–10, NIV

Understand I am *not* saying leaders should put on blinders and plug their ears as they plunge ahead. No one should make important decisions without soliciting input from trusted advisers. We need all available information when we make decisions, but we also need to have the courage to make decisions that may be unpopular and run counter to public opinion.

Remember, if you make decisions by not acting until you have the results of the latest public opinion survey, the next poll could be the one that replaces you!

Here's another principle for courageous leadership: *Be willing to advocate for your values.* In other words, be a person of conviction, and have the fortitude to stand up for what you believe.

I remember when I attended a very competitive professional military school where all the students were required to deliver a persuasive speech. We were allowed to pick any subject, but we had to strongly advocate our chosen stance, all in no less than nine minutes and thirty seconds and no longer than ten minutes and thirty seconds. If your speech didn't fall within those time limits, your grade for the speech slipped precariously.

I had done very well in the school and was recognized as one of the leaders of my class. I had judiciously shared my Christian beliefs but was also circumspect, considering the secular nature of the school. However, as I was brainstorming what my speech would be, I felt strongly led to give a flat-out, unvarnished testimony about my Christian faith.

I mentally argued with the Lord for days about this before finally surrendering to His will. I resolved that I would do what the Lord was convicting me to do. I prepared my speech carefully, prayed for receptive hearts among my classmates, and committed the outcome to God.

As I delivered that speech, I felt God's presence. About eight minutes into it, tears started to fill my eyes. I felt overwhelmed with what the Lord had done in my life and family, and I was unable to finish. I had "busted" the time limit and hadn't even finished what I wanted to say! As I returned to my seat, I felt embarrassed as tears continued to run down my cheeks.

But as I sat down and looked sheepishly around, I noticed many of my classmates' eyes were wet, too! Then someone said, "How do you give a grade to that speech?" Someone else answered, "I don't know, but the entire school needs to hear it. Let's send him to the school's speech contest."

The outcome was that not only was I privileged to share my testimony of Christ with the entire school, but I won the award for the top persuasive speech. As I look back, the award was inconsequential, but the lesson I learned was invaluable. I had learned to wisely advocate my values in spite of public pressure.

Number six on my courage list: *A courageous leader must not be afraid to express passion.*

Many of us labor under the misconception that the consummate leader keeps an iron grip on his emotions. And passion? Forget it! The epitome of leadership is to be cool, calm, and calculating—even uncaring and heartless—under pressure, right? Wrong.

Our values and beliefs as leaders *should* touch our hearts as well as our minds.

Contrary to the above stereotype of the "perfect leader," I have learned over the years to let my passion and emotions come out in a natural, healthy way. While wisdom and discipline certainly play their roles in godly leadership, the Lord wants us to use all that we are in our callings, and that includes the emotions and passions He has given us.

At first, this was very difficult for me. But as I read the gospel accounts of Jesus' ministry, I noticed that He actually was our model for godly expression of passion and emotions.

He wept when His friend Lazarus died; He got angry with the self-righteous religious leaders of His day; He hugged little children; He spoke sorrowfully when looking over the rebellious, yet suffering city of Jerusalem; He painfully prayed in the Garden of Gethsemane to be spared His bloody death (yet He surrendered His will to the Father's); He passionately told the disciples about His upcoming death and resurrection; He rebuked those same disciples for their unbelief after He had risen from the dead; and the Scripture implies He may have laughed often.

Jesus also made it clear He approved—actually, He blessed—loving, genuine displays of emotion and passion among His followers. Remember the story of Lazarus' sister, Mary, who took a pint of very expensive perfume, poured it on Jesus' feet, and began to wipe the Lord's feet with her hair? This extravagant display of raw, pure affection and worship stunned the disciples, and in the case of Judas Iscariot even stirred an angry retort. But Jesus saw Mary's actions for what they were—holy, humble love—and commended her for it. Read the account for yourself, and prayerfully insert yourself into this remarkable event:

Six days before the Passover, Jesus arrived at Bethany, where Lazarus lived, whom Jesus had raised from the dead. Here a dinner was given in Jesus' honor. Martha served, while Lazarus was among those reclining at the table with him. Then Mary took about a pint of pure nard, an expensive perfume; she poured it on Jesus' feet and wiped his feet with her hair. And the house was filled with the fragrance of the perfume.

But one of his disciples, Judas Iscariot, who was later to betray him, objected, "Why wasn't this perfume sold and the money given to the poor? It was worth a year's wages." He did not say this because he cared about the poor but because he was a thief; as keeper of the money bag, he used to help himself to what was put into it.

"Leave her alone," Jesus replied. "It was intended that she should save this perfume for the day of my burial. You will always have the poor among you, but you will not always have me."

—JOHN 12:1–8, NIV

For leaders and followers alike, there are many truths that can be taught from this passage of Scripture. I believe one of the most important lessons Jesus would have us learn is to give ourselves permission to express passion and healthy emotions. Let your heart express occasional tears, let the passion flavor your words, your laughter, the touch of your hands, and the expressions on your face!

Am I calling for unleashing an emotional tidal wave? Of course not. But emotions, properly channeled, season our interactions just like the right pinch of salt or dash of pepper heightens enjoyment of a good meal. It can be the same with leadership. This much is for certain: A passionless leader comes across as, at best, aloof, but more likely as uncaring—and thus is limited in his or her effectiveness.

I have also learned to become more passionate in my expression of love to Jesus Christ. This was contrary to my naturally reserved nature, but I have learned that there are times when tears, emotion-laden phrases of adoration, hands raised in praise, bowing, kneeling, or just being lovingly silent before the Lord become both simple and eloquent forms of worship.

However you meet the Lord, make it truly heart-to-heart! Bottom line: The love of Christ should touch our minds, bodies, and emotions. Honesty and humility are the keys. Consider this parable of Jesus as a perfect illustration:

> "Two men went up to the temple to pray, one a Pharisee and the other a tax collector. The Pharisee stood and prayed thus with himself, 'God, I thank You that I am not like other men— extortioners, unjust, adulterers, or even as this tax collector. I fast twice a week; I give tithes of all that I possess.' And the tax collector, standing afar off, would not so much as raise his eyes to heaven, but beat his breast, saying, 'God, be merciful to me a sinner!'"
>
> —Luke 18:10–13

In most sermons you may hear about this parable, the theme relates to the purity and grace of God's righteousness compared to our thin, hopelessly sin-stained self-righteousness. But look deeper and I believe you will see, as I have, another truth: We are, like the tax collector, to be passionate in our expressions to God.

Religion by itself does not touch the heart, but a personal relationship with God does. Once our hearts are touched, our expression of love and gratitude to God are free to gush out.

Number seven: *Godly leaders courageously share their faith.*

I know what you must be thinking: *This is a tricky proposition.* You are right; it can be very awkward for a leader to share his beliefs. You never want to use your position of authority to pressure your subordinates over matters of faith. But neither can we be true to our Lord and also afraid or ashamed to speak out for the Good News when we have an appropriate opportunity.

In my thirty years of service as an Air Force officer, I shared my faith on many occasions with peers, superiors, and subordinates alike. Most often, these exchanges grew directly out of questions someone would ask me. But what followed was a natural conversation without any preaching or pressure on my part. Never did anyone I talked to about my faith in Christ ever accuse me of forcing my beliefs upon them.

Opportunities to share our faith need not be forced. They flow from how we live, which informs our actions and creates a natural platform from which to speak. If we live our lives in ways consistent with the faith we profess, people will want to know why we are the way we are—and they will ask.

Meanwhile, we need to ask God to touch people's lives by expressing His love through us, and we need to seek heavenly wisdom to know when and how to share God's love with others.

Here is how the Apostle Peter put it:

> Quietly trust yourself to Christ your Lord, and if anybody asks why you believe as you do, be ready to tell him, and do it in a gentle and respectful way.
>
> —1 PETER 3:15, TLB

REFLECTIONS

Ask God to help you to be a courageous leader in the following areas:

- Lord, help me to admit to others when I have a need or problem.

- Lord, help me to stand up for the underdog, even when no one else will.

- Lord, help me to speak out when something is not right. Give me wisdom to speak with conviction and grace.

- Lord, help me to be humble enough to admit when I am wrong. Use me as a model to those I lead.

- Lord, help me to be different from the crowd by making the right decision even if it isn't popular.

- Lord, please help me to stand up for the values you have built into my life.

- Lord, help me to be a passionate leader. Use me to touch the hearts and minds of others. May I never be ashamed to express healthy emotions and the passion You have put in my heart.

- Finally, Lord, help me to share my Christian faith with others. First, touch them with the way I live my life, and second, give me wise and loving words when You give me the opportunity to speak.

Remember: *Courage is not a feeling; it starts with a decision to do the right thing.* If you earnestly asked God to help you in the above areas, I believe He will give you the power you need to carry out your decisions.

People are looking for leaders who stand up for what they believe and walk in godly character. They will gladly follow leaders of courage!

Chapter Six

THE GRACE OF THE LEADER

I F YOU ARE paying attention, life will inevitably teach you about grace. And while these experiences in life's classroom can vary widely in detail, I believe the lessons learned typically fall into three foundational categories.

The first one, actually, inspired my selection of the title for this book: *The Grace Goes With the Chair*. See if this example from my life that I briefly shared in the Introduction to this book resonates with you. At one point in my military career, I found myself being groomed to replace a respected, highly effective officer in a particularly challenging assignment. I remember clearly the sinking feeling I had as I watched him do his job—a job that was soon to be mine. I was amazed how he handled the many difficult meetings, phone calls, and other demands.

The more I saw of him in action, the more I felt totally inadequate.

Does this sound familiar to you?

The second category? Let's call that one *knowing what to do when elephants show up at your door*. As a young officer, I was selected for a special training program in the Pentagon. Along with one hundred other officers, I worked on the prestigious Air Staff for one year. I was rotated through many staff assignments and given a variety of challenging tasks and responsibilities.

On one occasion, I led a study aimed at resolving some serious military contracting problems. When I was given this assignment, I panicked. My mind was swirling with doubts about my abilities to get this job done. I had no expertise in this area, and it all seemed so *big*. I did not know even where to start!

Have you ever felt so overwhelmed that you were frozen in your tracks for fear of taking the next step?

The third principle in the struggle to fill those seemingly oversized shoes of responsibility: *The bigger the chair, the bigger the serving of grace.*

How about you? When is the last time you faced a problem so big that you didn't have a clue about where to even begin addressing it? I experienced this truth at a point in my career where I was leading a very large organization. I felt like I was just barely keeping my head above water, let alone being able to figuratively swim toward successful conclusions to the challenges facing me at the time.

Fortunately, I had an extremely capable boss willing to listen—to be a sounding board for my uncertainties. His experience and advice helped me see better the path ahead of me. On more than one occasion, I thought, *I bet he would know just what to do with this issue. It will be nice when I come to a point in my life when I will be just like him.*

So, let's dive deeper into these situations. I will share with you the insights I gained going through them and some biblical examples from the lives of two Old Testament heroes: Moses and Gideon.

THE GRACE GOES WITH THE CHAIR

First, consider two working definitions I will depend on as we explore this first principle. *Grace* encompasses your access to all of God's resources to empower you as you step into His will for your future as a leader. The *chair* represents the responsibilities God puts into your hands.

Expect to feel overwhelmed; you are not alone.

Let's face it, we all feel overwhelmed as leaders from time to time (maybe more times than not). Remember the Old Testament story about Gideon? The Book of Judges, chapter 6, recounts how the Lord visited Gideon and called him to a position of military leadership:

> And the Angel of the Lord appeared to him, and said to him, "The Lord is with you, you mighty man of valor!"
> —JUDGES 6:12

Wow, that's quite an endorsement, isn't it? There was just one problem: Gideon was a farmer with little or no battlefield experience. When the Lord addressed him as a warrior of renown, Gideon was shocked. What could he possibly do to save Israel from an invading army? After all, Gideon was the same guy who had just moments before been hiding inside a wine press, secretly threshing his wheat where Midianite raiders couldn't steal it!

I know there have been times when I've felt just like Gideon did when a new, seemingly mountainous challenge loomed in my path. You know the feeling: *Oh, yes—that new "chair" looks awfully big; I wonder if my legs, figuratively, would even reach the floor, or just dangle off the edge!*

I have found myself on the other end of that experience, too, as the veteran leader introducing younger officers to their own new "chairs." I remember once meeting with six fledgling lieutenants who had just been assigned to my organization. This time, *I* was a seasoned colonel, the guy able to draw on a wealth of leadership experiences.

As I spoke with these new officers, I could see, despite their best efforts to put on confident, brave fronts, that they were feeling staggered by what faced them. Could they live up to what the Air Force was expecting of them? Could they live up to what *I* would expect of them?

That was when I told them something they never expected to hear from their leader. I told them matter-of-factly that I, too, often felt overwhelmed by responsibilities and expectations. *They were shocked.*

In fact, I told them there was *not a day* I could remember where some new problem or responsibility had not caused me to feel like I had suddenly been buried under a landslide. Then I told them how they could dig themselves out—how they could deal with these feelings of inadequacy.

The point is that everyone feels overwhelmed at times. The issue is how we deal with those feelings.

Here is what I shared with them, and now with you. I hope my insights will help.

God always gives you the needed grace.

Whenever you are given a new task or job, God's grace is there. You can count on it! That is what Gideon learned, though he took a lot of convincing. The Bible recounts how it wasn't enough for this frightened farmer-turned-reluctant-warrior to hear God's voice and see an angelic messenger; Gideon still had doubts when his sacrifice was miraculously consumed by fire that erupted from a rock.

So, he twice tested God with fleeces laid out overnight, the first time requiring the wool be wet come daybreak while the ground around it be dry, and the second time that the fleece be dry while the ground around it be covered with morning dew.

Through all these "tests," God was patient. He knew Gideon needed the extra assurance in order to finally trust in Him. Gideon knew that when God said He would be with him and empower him to do what was asked, the Lord's word was pure gold!

Read this promise that God made to Gideon, and prayerfully apply it to yourself:

> The LORD turned to him and said, "Go in the strength you have and save Israel out of Midian's hand. Am I not sending you?"
>
> "But Lord," Gideon asked, "how can I save Israel? My clan is the weakest in Manasseh, and I am the least in my family."
>
> The Lord answered, "I will be with you, and you will strike down all the Midianites together."
>
> —JUDGES 6:14–16, NIV

Moses faced a similar challenge when he was trying to lead Israel into the Promised Land. There was, literally, a big problem: the inhabitants of Canaan included a fair number of *giants*. In fact, they looked unbeatable to ten of the twelve spies Moses had dispatched to reconnoiter this land God had promised was "flowing with milk and honey."

These "timid ten" could not look beyond the giants to the promise that God had repeatedly made and repeatedly demonstrated through miraculous provision and rescue to protect and provide for them.

"We seemed like grasshoppers in our own eyes, and we looked the same to them," they whined. Their fear of the giants spread panic throughout the camp, a veritable wildfire of fright that crippled Israel's faith. They could not see the promise; they could only see the looming problems.

The other two spies, Joshua and Caleb, clearly understood that God's grace would make a difference. They spoke boldly, frustrated with the attitudes of their brethren:

Joshua son of Nun and Caleb son of Jephunneh, who were among those who had explored the land, tore their clothes and said to the entire Israelite assembly, "The land we passed through and explored is exceedingly good. If the Lord is pleased with us, he will lead us into that land, a land flowing with milk and honey, and will give it to us. Only do not rebel against the Lord. And do not be afraid of the people of the land, because we will swallow them up. Their protection is gone, but the Lord is with us. Do not be afraid of them."

—NUMBERS 14:6–9, NIV

The promises made to Gideon and to Moses and Israel are really the same promises He makes to His children today: He *will* be with us; His grace *will* be there for us with all the resources needed to succeed in the mission He has given us—and that includes His power, His wisdom, His courage, His stamina, and His people to help us, too.

In whatever responsibilities you are facing, God will be with you. *His grace goes with the chair!*

The mantle of grace comes when you are in the chair, not before.

Earlier I shared how I felt overwhelmed when watching my boss do a job I was soon expected to take over. The reason I felt that way was because I simply did not yet have the grace to do it.

My boss had it, for sure. But as things turned out, that mantle of grace would be mine when I sat in that chair. We should never make up our minds about whether we can do something solely based on our current resources we have from God. If the Lord leads you to new challenges, those grace resources will be there when they are needed.

Being human, it is difficult *not* to try peering into the future…and worrying about what *might* happen and our inability to handle what *may* come. In such fearful imaginings, we see ourselves as alone, trying to tread water in storm-tossed seas.

Avoid that journey into a future only God knows and controls. Realize He gives you the grace for what you are doing *today,* and He will give you the grace for what He calls for you to do *tomorrow.*

Let me relate a story to illustrate this point. One day, I noticed that my deputy was watching me closely as I dealt with a very complex issue. In two months, he would assume my duties when I moved on to a new assignment. His face looked very troubled, and I could almost read his thoughts.

I told him, "I know what you are thinking. You doubt whether you would have had the wisdom to handle the situation I just faced. In fact, you are feeling inadequate about taking over in a few months."

His expression was one of shock. Then he exclaimed, "How did you know that?"

I quickly related the story of me watching the person I had replaced. I told him that I had felt the same way he was feeling now. Then I shared the lesson I had learned, that God's grace came with the chair. His once-troubled face took on a transformed countenance.

It comes down to trust. Do not be tempted to look at a "new chair" and then worry about how big it is and whether you can really sit in it. You will do just fine because *the grace comes with the chair*. If you look too far into the future or start comparing yourself to someone else, it's a guarantee: you will begin to feel overwhelmed.

Their grace is not *your* grace. *Your* grace is sufficient for *your* responsibilities, both now and in the future!

When the Apostle Paul was facing a seemingly impossible situation, he asked God to remove the circumstances. But God did not take Paul out of his circumstances; instead, God made a wonderful promise to him, and this same promise applies to each of us:

> Each time He said, "No. But I am with you; that is all you need. My power shows up best in weak people." Now I am glad to boast about how weak I am; I am glad to be a living demonstration of Christ's power, instead of showing off my own power and abilities.
>
> —2 Corinthians 12:9, TLB

The lives of Old Testament prophets Elijah and Elisha offer similar examples. Elisha followed Elijah for many months, watching how the older man of God ministered. Elisha, the Lord's chosen successor to Elijah, also must have wondered if he would be up to the assignment.

Don't you think Elisha had some doubts and felt inadequate as he watched his mentor? I am sure the answer is a resounding *yes!* Elisha was there when the older prophet was taken up to heaven, and Elisha received the promised mantle of prophetic authority.

Just like God expects us to sit in those new "chairs" with trust in His promise to empower us, Elisha made the decision to pick up and wear the mantle. God was faithful, using Elisha as powerfully as He had used Elijah. God will do the same for you.

Stand beside Elisha in your imagination during this critical moment in his life:

> Then it happened, as they continued on and talked, that suddenly a chariot of fire appeared with horses of fire, and separated the two of them; and Elijah went up by a whirlwind into heaven.
>
> And Elisha saw it, and he cried out, "My father, my father, the chariot of Israel and its horsemen!" So he saw him no more. And he took hold of his own clothes and tore them into two pieces. He also took up the mantle of Elijah that had fallen from him, and went back and stood by the bank of the Jordan. Then he took the mantle of Elijah that had fallen from him, and struck the water, and said, "Where is the Lord God of Elijah?" And when he also had struck the water, it was divided this way and that; and Elisha crossed over.
>
> —2 KINGS 2:11–14

If you complain, you may lose the mantle of grace.

With the blessing always comes a warning: Murmuring and complaining are grace killers. They tell God that you do not believe Him, and they certainly do not honor Him or edify you.

Israel murmured, complained, and rejected the pleas from Moses, Aaron, and the two faithful spies to ignore the giants and trust God's promises to go before them as they claimed their new homeland. When the children of Israel instead burrowed into their fears, God responded by removing the mantle of grace from these faithless complainers:

> The Lord said to Moses and Aaron: "How long will this wicked community grumble against me? I have heard the complaints of these grumbling Israelites. So tell them, 'As surely as I live, declares the Lord, I will do to you the very things I heard you say: In this desert your bodies will fall—every one of you

twenty years old or more who was counted in the census and who has grumbled against me. Not one of you will enter the land I swore with uplifted hand to make your home, except Caleb son of Jephunneh and Joshua son of Nun.'"

—Numbers 14:26–30, niv

How about you? Are you complaining about that new "chair" God has called you to sit in? *Stop.* You risk losing His grace for that challenge, that promotion, that bigger, better chance to serve the kingdom of God! Instead, ask the Lord right now for forgiveness for your lack of trust, and resolve, with His help, to go forward in His grace.

Go further than that. Ask forgiveness from the people who have heard your murmuring and complaining, too. Do not miss the grace of God due to foolish and selfish words. His grace is sufficient for you, now and forever. There are few greater joys than to see God's grace work in you to do what you thought was impossible!

When Elephants Show Up at Your Door

Let me introduce you to an elephant. OK, I'm not talking about a literal pachyderm using its trunk to thud on your front door or trumpeting its demands for attention and entry. These elephants are metaphorical—those big problems we all face, the unexpected challenges that barge into our lives that just cannot be ignored.

As you stand in the shadow of these elephants, their ears flapping hot wind into your eyes, their bulk and swinging tusks blocking your way, you feel paralyzed. What do you do with an elephant at the door? Run? Hide? Shut the door and hope it can't just nudge that glue-and-plywood flat with a single kick? Feed the beast a couple buckets of peanuts?

Let me offer a few suggestions based on years of dealing with herds of elephants that tried to stampede through the doors of my office, my home and family, and every other door of my life.

Visits from elephants are not unusual.

The mammoth problems of life visit everyone; you are not unique! It just *seems* like you are the only one they visit when they do show up. Over time, I have learned to welcome them. I guess you could say I've made the front door quite a bit wider!

The truth is that God uses elephants to show us the sufficiency of His grace. He also uses them to grow and mature us. In fact, God promises in Scripture that He will never allow an elephant to visit that you cannot handle with His grace. Whether it is a temptation, a broken relationship, or a problem that seems totally impossible, God will make a way!

> No temptation has seized you except what is common to man. And God is faithful; he will not let you be tempted beyond what you can bear. But when you are tempted, he will also provide a way out so that you can stand up under it.
> —1 CORINTHIANS 10:13, NIV

So, quit feeling like you are the only one with big problems. *Elephants visit everyone.* The issue is, how are you going to feed and care for them? Here are four insights I have found helpful.

If you do not have to feed it right away, let the elephant wait.

Many times I have found that an elephant will find a way to feed itself. In other words, many problems solve themselves before you have to address them!

I am not saying don't worry, ignore the problem, and be happy. I am saying just don't feed an elephant before you have to. By their calling and their nature, leaders are busy. We each have a list of elephants that will have to be fed at some point, but we need to have a feeding schedule.

I cannot count the number of times I wrestled with a huge problem that did not have to be handled right away. I worried for a while and then was forced to focus my attention on other elephants that had to be fed. When I returned to the previous elephant, I often found that it had fed itself or had gone away.

After seeing this happen a few times, I started keeping a special folder on my desk. In it, I would file the "big problems" that did not immediately require my attention. I would review the file every day to make sure something was not slipping through the cracks, but I would not start working on the problem until I had to.

Amazingly, I found that over half of these "folder elephants" had fed themselves or gone away. For those that remained, I found that when I did decide to tackle that next big problem, I had a better perspective to deal with it.

I was often asked, "What is that file on your desk?" I would reply, "It is problems I don't have to solve right now, and I am confident that many of them will go away by themselves."

That comment would often generate a chuckle, and sometimes it was a matter of the listener laughing *at* me as well as *with* me. Nonetheless, I learned that many of these same folks went on to create similar files of their own. In other words, there were fewer elephants running wild out there, and more of them had been given manila cardboard reservations!

Some might dismiss this technique as thinly-disguised procrastination. *Not true.* I am generally not a procrastinator; I just discovered a wonderful tool to help me prioritize and better focus on big problems.

Focus on the first bite, not the whole meal.

The biggest problem in feeding elephants is just getting started. It is only natural that you may focus on the enormous appetite of an elephant rather than just beginning the feeding task. Rather than backing up the figurative dump truck to fill the elephant's trough, focus on the beast's first bite, or the first step you must take to address the problem.

What should be on the menu? What should that first step be, specifically? You probably won't know from your own experience, but others may have fed this particular elephant or one like it before. Ask them about that, and you will be amazed at the help you will get from just a few questions and their answers. All sorts of ideas may flow that clarify your next move; gather them, list them, and then pray. Ask the Lord what you need to do first, because He has promised to guide you:

> If you need wisdom—if you want to know what God wants you to do—ask him, and he will gladly tell you. He will not resent your asking.
>
> —JAMES 1:5, TLB

God *will* show you how to start.

Next, ask yourself if the elephant's meal can be divided into entrees or more easily handled pieces. This is another way of identifying other major steps you will need to take to overcome that problem. As those steps occur to you, though, just brainstorm them together. Don't be in a rush to prioritize them.

This commitment to prayerful, tactical thinking will help you arrange those entrees. (Appetizers, soup, and salad, after all, come before the main course—and you never start with dessert, right?) After the brainstorming is complete, put these major steps in some kind of order; the act of organizing your approach to the problem, by itself, can reduce stress considerably.

Now, having tapped God's wisdom, you have a plan, and you have taken the hardest step: that of getting started toward the solution.

Finally, ask one more question: "Is this an elephant I have to feed alone, or do I need a team?" If you need a team, then your brain-storming has given you some solid initial thoughts to share with them and to help them get started, too. Your first meeting will have focus and direction, and that sense of organization at the beginning can make all the difference.

Don't forget to say grace before you start the meal.

OK, you have a plan. God has given you wisdom. You are ready to start the meal. But are you really ready? I have learned to say "grace" before all such "meals." What do I mean? Well, I always thank God for the wisdom He has given, the wisdom I will still need, the people who have already helped, the people who will help, and for the flexibility to adjust once the actual elephant feeding starts.

Feeding times can get messy. Nothing ever goes as expected. Stay in an attitude of prayer and thanksgiving during the meal.

Be encouraged.

God will see you through the feeding of the elephant. Don't give in to panic if something goes awry. (Elephants can be picky eaters. In other words, unexpected twists and turns can pop up with any problem.) Instead, remember that elephant you fed a year ago. The hungry beast that looked so big then seems like a pygmy elephant now, right? God provided the solutions then, and He will do so now...and next year, this elephant at the door will also look like a toy stuffed animal!

THE BIGGER THE CHAIR, THE BIGGER THE SERVING OF GRACE

Earlier in this book, I told you about a boss I respected a great deal, one from whom I had often received good advice and direction. Whenever I was stumped, he always seemed to have the answers by drawing on his sharp mind and wealth of experience.

On one of my visits, though, I ended up with an unexpected perspective. I had come in, as I had before, to share some problems I was facing and get his feedback. This time, though, I ended up listening to him describe some of the issues *he* was facing—and they were huge!

As I left his office, I had a new appreciation and understanding for "chairs" that were bigger than my own. And with that glimpse into his world, I also gained an important insight: the bigger the chair, the bigger the elephants you will face.

This time, my boss was seeking my input on how best to deal with some of his troublesome pachyderms. I came away with a greater urgency to pray for my boss (more on this later) and a healthier perspective about my own problems.

I left that meeting convinced that I did not want my boss's job. But before that thought was fully out of my mind, another one followed—a revelation from God that has since proven to be a great help and assurance as I have assumed greater responsibilities over the years: *The bigger the chair you are given, the bigger the serving of God's grace that is given to you.*

In your lifetime you will, sadly, see leaders—both above you, and under you—who do not grasp or seek the promise of God's grace going with those "chairs" He truly gives us. I trust that you will be different, that *you* will realize that the bigger *your* chair, the more of God's power, wisdom, courage, and stamina are available.

And consider this, too: When you flow with God's purpose and direction, when you sit in that new chair with confidence and trust in Him, you will find you have gained access to similarly devoted and inspired contacts who can help you and whom you can help!

However, it is important that as your particular chairs grow bigger, as you move into new positions of authority and responsibility, you don't forget your roots. Don't get impatient with a subordinate leader who asks your help with what now seems to you to be merely a pygmy elephant. Remember what it was like when you were in his chair. Be a teacher and encourager!

Finally, let me offer some tips for interacting with someone in a chair that is bigger than yours. First, ask if there is any way you can assist them. Just making the offer may make your superior's day!

"Do unto others as you would have them do unto you" is the Golden Rule that Jesus taught (see Matthew 7:12). This certainly applies to the challenges of leadership, mentoring, and humbly seeking wisdom alike: Those who give help to others in turn sow seeds to receive help from others.

Second, do not ask for help from a superior with one of your elephants until you have done all you can do to feed it. When you do approach the superior, share the following details about your "elephant":

What you have done to this point in trying to solve the problem.

Identify others who are helping you.

What possible solutions you have considered. (If I ever sensed that one of my subordinates had not really taken the problem as far as he could, I would ask him to do more homework and then return.)

Finally, don't ever try to give your elephants away to your boss or anyone else! God trusted them to you, and you have His mantle of grace to deal with them.

REFLECTIONS

- Thank God right now for the grace that always comes with the chairs He gives you.

- Ask God's forgiveness for sometimes looking too far into the future and foolishly comparing yourself to others who have a different mantle of grace.

- Thank God for the wisdom to feed every elephant that comes to you.

- Thank Him for showing you the first steps to take.

- Thank Him for open eyes to see others who can help you.

- Thank Him for showing you how to organize the feeding.

- Ask God to help you serve others with bigger chairs than yours.

- Commit to God that you will never again try to give one of your elephants away.

Chapter Seven

THE FLEXIBILITY OF THE LEADER

I F THERE IS one looming challenge for any leader—one that is constant, consistently unsettling, and yet abundantly filled with the potential for progress—it is *change.*

Whether you fear it, run from it, anticipate it, embrace it, or just try not to think about it, change is inevitable. Consider these quotations, serious and tongue-in-cheek, for some perspective:

> The great thing is, if one can, to stop regarding all the unpleasant things as interruptions in one's "own" or "real" life. The truth is, of course, that what one regards as interruptions are precisely one's life.
>
> —C.S. LEWIS

> We cannot change our past. We cannot change the fact that people act in a certain way. We cannot change the inevitable. The only thing we can do is play on the one string we have, and that is our attitude.
>
> —CHARLES SWINDOLL

> If you're in a bad situation, don't worry it'll change. If you're in a good situation, don't worry it'll change.
>
> —JOHN A. SIMONE, SR.

We are living in times where change is occurring in almost every technological, political, and social arena of our existence. In fact, it seems the rate of change is only accelerating, and leaders are required to be more and more flexible about how they relate to their superiors and staff and how they do their jobs and with what tools.

The pace of change can be downright dizzying! Some leaders love handling change, but most of us don't relish handling these tsunamis of so-called progress. The latter frame of mind perfectly describes me early in my leadership life.

I hated change. Change stirred up all the insecurities within me. It has taken God's miraculous grace—and my willingness to put in the hard work to change my attitude toward change—to arrive at the point where I am today, where I embrace change as healthy.

Old Testament patriarchs like Abraham and Moses became experts in handling the enormous changes God demanded of them—changes that turned their worlds upside down and sideways!

For Abraham, hearing God's voice and obeying His call meant massive upheaval. Before the Lord was through with him, he would have a new name (he started out as Abram, or "exalted father," and was renamed by God Abraham, or "father of multitudes"); would be wandering far from his home in the Babylonian city of Ur into the strange tracts of Canaan to the west; would uproot himself and his family from the clan ties and culture they had grown up with; and would devote himself to the one Creator, rather than the many gods that tradition says his father, an idol merchant, believed in:

> The LORD had said to Abram, "Leave your country, your people and your father's household and go to the land I will show you. I will make you into a great nation and I will bless you; will make your name great, and you will be a blessing. I will bless those who bless you, and whoever curses you I will curse; and all peoples on earth will be blessed through you." So Abram left, as the LORD had told him; and Lot went with him. Abram was seventy-five years old when he set out from Haran. He took his wife Sarai, his nephew Lot, all the possessions they had accumulated and the people they had acquired in Haran, and they set out for the land of Canaan, and they arrived there.
>
> —GENESIS 12:1–5, NIV

Moses endured enormous changes in his life, too. First, his desperate family set him adrift in a basket on the Nile, hoping and praying their child could escape the infanticide ordered by Pharaoh for all Jewish male children. He was saved by Pharaoh's daughter and raised as royalty. He became a fugitive after killing an abusive Egyptian slave overseer. And after what must have been a brutal crossing of the Sinai, he settled down as a lowly shepherd for Jethro, who soon became his father-in-law.

Talk about a roller coaster! But Moses' wild ride was just beginning, for he had an appointment with God—and a call to leadership, with a capital "L":

> Now Moses was tending the flock of Jethro his father-in-law, the priest of Midian, and he led the flock to the far side of the desert and came to Horeb, the mountain of God. There the angel of the LORD appeared to him in flames of fire from within a bush. Moses saw that though the bush was on fire it did not burn up. So Moses thought, "I will go over and see this strange sight—why the bush does not burn up."
>
> When the LORD saw that he had gone over to look, God called to him from within the bush, "Moses! Moses!"
>
> And Moses said, "Here I am."
>
> "Do not come any closer," God said. "Take off your sandals, for the place where you are standing is holy ground." Then he said, "I am the God of your father, the God of Abraham, the God of Isaac and the God of Jacob." At this, Moses hid his face, because he was afraid to look at God.
>
> The LORD said, "I have indeed seen the misery of my people in Egypt. I have heard them crying out because of their slave drivers, and I am concerned about their suffering. So I have come down to rescue them from the hand of the Egyptians and to bring them up out of that land into a good and spacious land, a land flowing with milk and honey—the home of the Canaanites, Hittites, Amorites, Perizzites, Hivites and Jebusites. And now the cry of the Israelites has reached me, and I have seen the way the Egyptians are oppressing them. So now, go. I am sending you to Pharaoh to bring my people the Israelites out of Egypt....
>
> "The elders of Israel will listen to you. Then you and the elders are to go to the king of Egypt and say to him, 'The Lord, the God of the Hebrews, has met with us. Let us take a three-day journey into the desert to offer sacrifices to the Lord our

God.' But I know that the king of Egypt will not let you go unless a mighty hand compels him. So I will stretch out my hand and strike the Egyptians with all the wonders that I will perform among them. After that, he will let you go."
—EXODUS 3:1–10, 18–20, NIV

Abraham and Moses are viewed today as mighty men of God, almost as superhumans compared to us. Miracles and blessings flowed through and from their lives. But it is easy to forget these were still just *men*, subject to the same frailties as we are today. The truth is, sometimes these heroes of our faith responded well to the changes God brought their way, and sometimes they reacted poorly.

Abraham moved his entire family across hundreds of miles of dangerous territory. He had no significant help from others and had to rely on camels (no U-Hauls back then!) to make the journey. In terms of possessions, support of his clan, social and economic status, and even friends, Abraham and his small band of servants and livestock had to start over. In other words, Abraham, in following God's directions, found himself at the bottom of the proverbial pecking order of his time.

Abraham had to grow into his faith, too. Change is tough to deal with when it takes you into unfamiliar, scary territory. Repeatedly, he compromised in his obedience to God's commands, only partially following them. As a consequence, he had to repeat the lessons of trust the Lord was trying to teach him.

Moses may have gotten an "A" for intentions, but he got a resounding "F" for his initial attempts to answer the call to deliver his people. In his zeal and passion, he acted on impulse, killing that slave driver. Yes, Moses had failed miserably, ending up in hiding, herding sheep in a remote desert hick town.

Even when God directly called him, Moses argued he was not up to the task. *Hey, I tried this before. Why would I want to fail again? I'm better off staying here in Midian, far away from the Pharaoh and safe!* he probably thought to himself.

However reluctantly, Moses steeled himself and responded to God's call. The Lord's instructions were punctuated with some very strange methods: a series of devastating plagues on the Egyptians, supernatural pillars of fire and smoke, and a walking staff that turned into a snake and could part large bodies of water.

How about you? How do you respond to change? Maybe you hate change. You like things to just stay the same, with everything in its right place. You rarely, if ever, try anything new, and you resent people who introduce new ideas. In fact, you are very disciplined and predictable.

On the other hand, perhaps you love the new and novel. You are easily bored, and you often stir the pot to just get things moving. Change gets your juices going, and you love the adventure of change.

Regardless of where you are on the spectrum of embracing change, there are five key areas of change that we all must face and conquer to move forward as godly leaders. It is extremely important that we handle them well.

FIVE AREAS OF CHANGE CRITICAL TO YOUR SUCCESS

1. Dealing with a change in leaders.

An old French proverb, quoted by many luminaries over the centuries, goes like this: "The more things change, the more they stay the same." In other words, the only thing constant about change is change itself. That is certainly true of leadership. Just when you get used to the boss, teacher, pastor, coach, etc., you have now, a new one comes on the horizon.

Suddenly, all the rules have changed. We have all been there. I particularly remember a challenging change in bosses that occurred.

Both men were good leaders in their own right, but their styles were radically different, and I much preferred the way the old boss did things. The old boss was a "big picture" kind of leader, one who didn't, as the saying goes, "sweat the small stuff." Instead, he left the details to trusted subordinates. He would dig just deep enough to get a handle on the matter before him and then make a decision. He let his staffers do the jobs he had given them. He avoided hovering over them as they did their work.

His successor, though, was far more devoted to the details. He would not make a decision until he had deeply explored all possibilities and personally vetted the suggested solutions. Once he did make a decision, he monitored the implementation by his subordinates.

On one occasion, one of this leader's frustrated key subordinates called me and asked advice on how to respond to this new leader's hands-on approach. While I understood how this subordinate felt, my best advice was uncompromising: I told him to quit chafing under the new leadership style and just give the new boss what he wanted.

"You are dealing with a new boss, and you will have to be prepared to give him a lot more detail when you discuss issues with him. He is not going to change; you will have to change," I told the subordinate.

There will always be changes at the top. It does no good to get angry or resentful or hope that the new leader will miraculously become like the old one. Further, it is the height of foolishness to compare the new leader to the old one. God made each leader to be unique. Each leader brings a fresh perspective and style to the table; more often than not, that's how growth—and progress—come into being.

On a flexibility scale of 1 to 10, with 10 being very flexible, how do you score when a new leader shows up? Do you try to do things the way the previous boss preferred? Do you support or try to undermine the change in leadership? Do you smile in the new leader's presence and grumble when he or she is not there?

God is interested in how we respond to leadership changes. All authority is established by God, and when we rebel, we are rebelling against God. Listen to the instruction Paul gave to believers so long ago:

> Everyone must submit himself to the governing authorities, for there is no authority except that which God has established. The authorities that exist have been established by God. Consequently, he who rebels against the authority is rebelling against what God has instituted, and those who do so will bring judgment on themselves. For rulers hold no terror for those who do right, but for those who do wrong. Do you want to be free from fear of the one in authority? Then do what is right and he will commend you. For he is God's servant to do you good. But if you do wrong, be afraid, for he does not bear the sword for nothing. He is God's servant, an agent of wrath to bring punishment on the wrongdoer. Therefore, it

is necessary to submit to the authorities, not only because of possible punishment but also because of conscience.

—ROMANS 13:1–5, NIV

A number of years ago, we made a very prayerful change in the worship style in our church. The new worship leader's style and selections were much different from our previous ones, and many in the church bristled at the change. In fact, the first year of the new worship agenda was downright *painful* for some of our people. They longed for the old style and older songs of worship. Some actually left the church.

Most, however, embraced the change and saw the positive impact it had on our congregation. At the end of two years, this new worship pastor was called to another church as the senior pastor. Most who had initially complained about him ended up in tears when he departed.

Almost always, the issues that arise with a new leader are not merely because he or she and their styles are different from the old; the *real* issue is our attitude about the change. The right attitude helps us to receive from the new leader; the right attitude makes the transition easier and enables God to work more fully in our lives.

In short, get used to it! As sure as the sun rises and sets, the tides come in and go out, and every April 15 your federal income taxes come due, you *will* have a variety of new leaders come into your life in the years ahead.

2. Starting over.

Moses had to start over again, again, and again. He tumbled from a cushy spot in Pharaoh's palace to keeping sheep and fetching water for goats and camels in the boonies. Then Moses went from being a superb shepherd to being a rejected leader. Think about it: He slid from acclaim to shame, and then went from watching fleece to having no peace.

You too will likely have to start over again and again. This happens when you move to a new town, start a new job, move into a new neighborhood, join a new church, or go to a new school. You have to make new friends, prove yourself, and totally readjust.

My own family moved fifteen times in the Air Force and twice (as of the time I write this) in the ministry. This meant new friends, new jobs, new neighborhoods, new houses, new schools, new churches, new geography, and umpteen other new things. In fact, in some areas we had to not only start over but start over from the bottom.

To take steps forward, we often had to take some steps that seemed like they were going backward. But in all that, this has always been true: God used these new starts to change, grow, and make us stronger!

Starting over means making decisions about how we accept and implement the changes that must be made. Will we try to learn and grow? Will we become resentful? Will be become jealous of others who appear further up the ladder? Again, it will be our attitude that proves to be the vital ingredient.

3. Having to turn right when you planned on going straight.

When Israel was marching toward the Promised Land, they came to the land of Edom. It belonged to a distant relative's offspring. Israel asked permission to pass through this land, hoping to avoid a circuitous detour that would take them into some very difficult terrain. Even though the Israelites promised not to take any water or food from Edom, they were refused entry. Talk about having to go right when you planned on going straight!

Here's the biblical account:

> Moses sent messengers from Kadesh to the king of Edom, saying:
> "This is what your brother Israel says: You know about all the hardships that have come upon us. Our forefathers went down into Egypt, and we lived there many years. The Egyptians mistreated us and our fathers, but when we cried out to the Lord, he heard our cry and sent an angel and brought us out of Egypt.
> "Now we are here at Kadesh, a town on the edge of your territory. Please let us pass through your country. We will not go through any field or vineyard, or drink water from any well. We will travel along the king's highway and not turn to the right or to the left until we have passed through your territory."
> But Edom answered:
> "You may not pass through here; if you try, we will march out and attack you with the sword."

The Israelites replied:

"We will go along the main road, and if we or our livestock drink any of your water, we will pay for it. We only want to pass through on foot—nothing else."

Again they answered: "You may not pass through."

Then Edom came out against them with a large and powerful army. Since Edom refused to let them go through their territory, Israel turned away from them.

—NUMBERS 20:14–21, NIV

There will be many times you, too, will have to take a difficult detour from what had seemed the logical, most efficient course. I speak from much experience in this. I have worked diligently on projects and laid detailed plans only to have a boss completely change direction or just say no and order me back to the drawing board.

Such delays or refusals made my job seem almost impossible at times. In fact, it seemed like these changes in direction often made no sense. I wanted to go back and argue the boss's final answer.

Sometimes I got angry and stewed in my own juices for days. But eventually, I learned some valuable lessons from these experiences, even when the boss was occasionally wrong. First, I learned that my plans were not to be chiseled in stone. I needed to be open to feedback and willing to modify any directions I had planned. Second, I needed to remember that I was serving God in these situations, even when things did not happen in the manner I had wished.

I am sure that more than a few Israelites were grumbling when they had to go around Edom, forced to take a very difficult and dangerous diversion.

When we are diverted from the path we had planned, though, we often see God's wisdom in the change of direction later on. We learn that He was protecting us from consequences we could not see; we discover the seemingly illogical detour was actually a better way to go...or the lesson may turn out simply to be one of flexibility.

That was the case for me when, as a young Air Force officer, I was assigned to attend the University of California at Los Angeles to earn a master's degree in business. During this assignment, God beautifully blessed my life, as well as my wife Debbe's life. We had high hopes that our subsequent assignment also would be in California, so with that in mind, I called a senior officer acquaintance that had some influence in the Air Force personnel system.

He agreed to help. Everything about this request—to both of us— seemed so logical, a win-win situation for me, then a young lieutenant with a family, and the Air Force, as well. It was, to our surprise, not to be. The acquaintance later called me to say he was unable to get me a California posting; instead, Debbe and I were heading to the opposite end of the country, Georgia.

You've probably heard the joke about the term "military intelligence" being an oxymoron? I was convinced of that being the case then; I was flabbergasted, frustrated, and furious at the decision. Here I had prayed earnestly that God would give us favor with an assignment in California, and instead God was sending us about as far away from California as one could get and still be in the United States!

But when you pray for God's favor, you need to be prepared for surprises. His ways indeed are not our ways!

Later on, Debbe and I recognized the Lord's great wisdom in having us "turn right instead of going straight." I received wonderful training in Georgia. We met a pastor who influenced my life more than any other individual. We made lifelong friends. God opened doors that would later lead to full-time ministry. And our marriage and family were profoundly and beautifully affected. I am so glad that I did not get my way!

4. Accepting new situations.

So, we have learned that, as the inventor Thomas Edison once said, "We shall have no better conditions in the future if we are satisfied with all those which we have at present." In other words, it's time to leave the comfort zone!

We will continually be challenged to do things we haven't done before. Our initial reaction is often, "There is no way I can do that." We watch others, compare ourselves to them, and want to run from the new situation.

What do you do when you are asked to speak in front of a crowd, visit a new place, confront an issue with a friend, deal with a different culture, or join a new group? Do you quickly say no? Do you get angry or defensive? Do you lie or make excuses? Do you criticize the thing you are being asked to do?

Or do you ask for help, try to learn, get involved even though it is uncomfortable, and be supportive, even though you would rather be somewhere else? That latter course is a much better one to choose. New situations deepen your dependence on God, broaden your horizons, and help you to grow in faith and confidence in areas where you have been stagnant.

Years ago, doors opened for me to minister in Honduras. I have had the privilege of sharing Gospel principles with many of the political and military leaders of that nation, including an appearance on a TV show with an audience of 3 million! But when this door first opened, I was reluctant to go. I sought the counsel of a friend from Africa, though, and he urged me to make the leap into this opportunity. I am so glad that I did not give in to the temptation to stay in my comfort zone. I have learned that comfort zones are prisons that lock you in and lock out opportunities.

5. Making new friends and accepting new people.

How can we ever fulfill Christ's Great Commission to take the Gospel to the world if we avoid meeting new people? I am ashamed to admit that at one time I was uncomfortable trying to reach out to strangers. No, actually, I avoided meeting new people whenever possible. I much preferred staying around those I already knew.

Now I am just the opposite. I might go out to golf alone and end up completing a foursome with complete strangers. Where before I may have just lurked behind a tree while they played through, now I find it fascinating to share with and learn about new people God brings into my path. I enjoy asking others questions.

When I think back to my former attitudes, I am amazed I was ever so "anti-social" when it came to strangers. What made me change? It was the love of God. His love came into my heart, and I, in turn, started seeing and loving others like He does.

What do you do when someone new comes into your group? Do you reach out to him or her and make them feel welcome? Do you relish learning about him or introducing her to others? Or do you watch from a distance, focused on the newcomer's clothes and looks, and feel resentful that someone new is infringing on "your territory"?

What happens when *you* are the new person in the group? Do you try and meet others, participate in their activities, and share willingly about yourself? Or do you wait for others to reach out to you, feel sorry for yourself, and get angry when others don't try to bring you into the fellowship?

God loves people, and we need to take on His perspective. His perspective is liberating!

REFLECTIONS

How do you respond to change in each of these five areas? Your responses will determine success or failure in various aspects of your life.

- Health

- Promotions

- Friendships

- Outcome of group endeavors

- Availability for God to use you

Some thoughts to consider...

- There will be many leadership changes in your life.

- There are no perfect leaders.

- You can learn from every leader.

- Each leader is unique.

- A good attitude will go a long way.

- First impressions are usually wrong. Reserve judgment.

- If you are unwilling to start over, you will never get ahead.

- The speed of your recovery from starting over is directly related to your acceptance of change.

- God will often ask you to take a step backward so you can take future steps forward.

- Never make plans and treat them like they are written in stone. Most of your plans will have to be modified.

- The modifications often bring better results.

- Be willing to change your plans and listen to others.

- New situations help grow and stretch you.

- You cannot avoid new situations.

- God wants you to learn new ways.

- God wants you to be more flexible.

- To make friends, you have to be friendly.

- Jesus reached out continually to new people.

- God expects you to love others like He loves them. Ask for God's love.

- Give God the right to bring change to any area of your life.

- Tell Him you give permission right now.

- He wants to be Lord of all your life.

Chapter Eight

THE FOCUS OF THE LEADER

THE GOSPELS RECOUNT four specific times where Jesus healed the blind, though there may have been many more. If you count the Apostle Paul's restoration of sight through prayer after being blinded and converted on the road to Damascus (as recounted in the Book of Acts), there were at least five such miracles. And who can count the healings of visually impaired believers in the centuries since that were attributed to the risen Christ?

Jesus physically healed the blind, but more importantly He sought, and still seeks today, to open spiritual eyes to His promised forgiveness, salvation, blessing and purpose. And He wants us to see clearly—to be able to focus on the path He has put before us.

For example, when Jesus healed a blind man in Bethsaida (Mark 8:23–25), He was not satisfied with the results of His first blessing of the man. Initially, the man could see, but not clearly. The man described seeing men walking, but "like trees"—he was not able to focus. A second blessing completed the miracle; the man's focus was clear, and his vision was then perfect.

Focus in seeing was important to Jesus then and now, especially as it applies to our spiritual eyes. Consider the Lord's Sermon on the Mount, which contained one particularly powerful illustration:

> "The eye is the lamp of the body. If your eyes are good, your whole body will be full of light. But if your eyes are bad, your whole body will be full of darkness. If then the light within you is darkness, how great is that darkness!"
>
> —MATTHEW 6:22–23, NIV

Your vision is critical to following Christ and being a godly leader, but your focus is vital. To see clearly with your spiritual eyes is one thing; to have the discipline to focus that sight on the right kind of scenery, though, makes all the difference.

Focus on the right things, and you will be blessed. Focus on the wrong things, and those blessings will evaporate like rainfall in California's Death Valley desert.

I believe God's desire for us to develop proper focus for our vision can be expressed in six determinations. Take on these goals the Lord has taught me as your own, and you will be blessed.

Determine That Everything You Do Is Part of Your Calling From God

Let's start with a working definition of what we mean by the term "calling." Your calling is all that God has planned for you, including everything that you do and every aspect of your life. Here is what the Bible has to say about it:

> Whatever your hand finds to do, do it with all your might, for in the grave, where you are going, there is neither working nor planning nor knowledge nor wisdom.
>
> —Ecclesiastes 9:10, niv

> So whether you eat or drink or whatever you do, do it all for the glory of God.
>
> —1 Corinthians 10:31, niv

> And whatever you do, whether in word or deed, do it all in the name of the Lord Jesus, giving thanks to God the Father through him.
>
> —Colossians 3:17, niv

This idea of putting God and His calling first in every part of your life runs completely contrary to the formulas for success taught today by many of the world's time, task, and goal management gurus. Let me give you an example.

When I was a young Air Force captain, a senior officer told me I needed to learn how to compartmentalize my life. His answer to life's competing and often conflicting demands was to wall himself off into each of his roles.

For example, he had his work compartment. Then, there was the family compartment, the recreational compartment, the spiritual compartment, and many others. The key, he said, was to focus only on one compartment at a time and not to allow these separate areas to bleed into each other. Don't take your family worries to the workplace; keep recreational and spiritual beliefs out of the office, too. When recreating, make that your sole focus, and ditto for each of the other "compartments."

Anyway, that's how his advice went. You get the picture. There were some aspects of this formula that were probably worth some thought. But for me, the compartmentalizing approach just didn't live up to my Savior's endorsement—and certainly didn't work for me.

First, his spiritual beliefs, compartmentalized as they were, did not seem to have real impact—at least, not a decisive impact that I was convinced should be the case—on the conduct of his family or work life.

Second, God had been impressing upon me that I was to see *everything* I do as part of my calling from Him. Again, He didn't want me to leave Him out of any of the so-called compartments.

I am convinced we need to bring God into everything in our lives. He should be the prime focus and ultimate motivator for us at work, at home with the wife and kids, at play, in building friendships, in pursuing personal and career goals, and even in our thought lives. Whatever I do or say should seek to reflect the glory of God.

Most men naturally compartmentalize their lives and tend to focus on one thing at a time. The challenge for us is to think and act differently, against our nature and more in tune with God's nature, to bring the Lord's glory (and thus, His blessings) into all our "compartments."

If you are a Christian, you should see everything you do as part of your calling. Never consider some parts of your life set aside as only secular and others exclusively spiritual. To God, it is all spiritual.

Think about it. If the Lord sees everything in life as being imbued with an overarching spiritual component, then shouldn't we? Realizing this truth led me to a determination to be a representative of Jesus Christ no matter what I was doing—working, playing, being with my family, or whatever.

In other words, I decided to try to live every aspect of my life just as if Jesus was standing right next to me physically. If you are a believer,

THE GRACE GOES WITH THE CHAIR

that should not be impossible, since Christ is with us spiritually, and that is no less real!

I regularly run into folks who raise their eyebrows when they learn that before I was a pastor, I spent thirty years as an Air Force officer. *That must be quite a tough transition, right?* Absolutely not! That is because I pursued my Air Force service as unto the Lord. I saw my military career as part of my calling, just as I now see being a pastor as part of my calling in living life as a serious Christian leader.

God does not see one calling as better than another calling. Here is what the Apostle Paul wrote about this truth of divine perception:

> The eye cannot say to the hand, "I don't need you!" And the head cannot say to the feet, "I don't need you!" On the contrary, those parts of the body that seem to be weaker are indispensable, and the parts that we think are less honorable we treat with special honor. And the parts that are unpresentable are treated with special modesty, while our presentable parts need no special treatment. But God has combined the members of the body and has given greater honor to the parts that lacked it, so that there should be no division in the body, but that its parts should have equal concern for each other. If one part suffers, every part suffers with it; if one part is honored, every part rejoices with it.
>
> Now you are the body of Christ, and each one of you is a part of it.
>
> —1 CORINTHIANS 12:21–27, NIV

Here's what I see as the core message of these scriptures: No calling is more important or spiritual than another calling. If it is done unto the Lord, it is spiritual. If it is done in a way to bless others, it is spiritual.

Some Americans may wince at this concept. Sadly, it has become commonplace in the United States to look down our noses at certain jobs or callings. In sports, everyone wants to be the ace baseball pitcher, not the third-string left-fielder; no one chases the spot of that end-of-the-bench basketball player who only sees action in practices but aspires to being the hot-shooting superstar; in football, who would rather block on the line than run the ball or throw the touchdown pass?

The same mind-set dominates the workplace. Blue-collar workers who toil with their hard, callused hands seem somehow more expendable than the white-collar, suit-wearing office executives with soft, manicured fingers.

And yes, in the church, isn't that pastor or worship leader naturally more spiritual than the fellow in the pews who quietly runs a good, honest business? Isn't that soloist with the angelic voice on the Sunday stage obviously more blessed that those who serve quietly in the background, collecting offerings, cleaning the church sanctuary and restrooms, or watching over the children in the nursery?

Whether we sing arias to heaven or change diapers, stir the soul with sermons or vacuum the carpets, God sees every part of our church body as important. We cannot take credit for any of the gifts or callings we have. They all come from God, our Creator. The only thing we can do is to use our gifts to the glory of God.

I remember a conversation I had with a close friend a number of years ago. He owned a business that employed almost twenty people. I was so impressed with his business that I commented it would be enjoyable to be part of his company.

He was shocked, taken aback by the fact that I would even consider being in his business. "You have a master's degree, and I have no education beyond high school," he sputtered, as if that difference between us truly meant something. In essence, he considered his business below my work experience.

It took some time, but I eventually convinced him that I believed his business was just as important as any job I had done. Many people with master's degrees fail in business. They would be jealous of his success and skill. Further, the impact of his business was far greater than he realized. Profitable and run with integrity, it provided for his family and for the families of his employees, who respected him and could be proud of their products. And his business gave him a priceless platform from which to model and share Christ.

My friend had fallen into a trap that so many of us stumble into: placing more value on certain callings than others. How about you? Do you understand that God does not see one calling as better than another?

After all, Jesus taught that God's rewards for the "five-talent person" and the "two-talent person" are the same. His parable here tells us that God rewards us for our diligence in using what He has given to us:

> "So he who had received five talents came and brought five other talents, saying, 'Lord, you delivered to me five talents; look, I have gained five more talents besides them.' His lord said to him, 'Well done, good and faithful servant; you were faithful over a few things, I will make you ruler over many things. Enter into the joy of your lord.' He also who had received two talents came and said, 'Lord, you delivered to me two talents; look, I have gained two more talents besides them.' His lord said to him, 'Well done, good and faithful servant; you have been faithful over a few things, I will make you ruler over many things. Enter into the joy of your lord.'"
>
> —MATTHEW 25:20–23

There are foundational principles of integrity, faithfulness, and responsible conduct in that parable, but there is another gem of a lesson that often goes unexplored: the call for godly leaders to validate their subordinates' accomplishments and their importance to the team.

The boss in the story Jesus told is the leader He wants us to imitate. He is not stingy with praise ("Well done!"), recognition ("good and faithful servant"), or specifics on accomplishments ("you have been faithful with a few things"), nor rewarding that faithfulness with further trust and challenges ("I will make you ruler over many things").

Is there any question that after hearing these words, these servants had any doubts about their importance to the team? They are clear on their lord's perspective that everyone is valuable and that the team only works when everyone is contributing their part.

SEE YOUR CURRENT RESPONSIBILITIES AS GOD'S TOOL TO SHAPE YOU FOR MORE RESPONSIBILITIES

As a young officer just a couple years out of the Air Force Academy, I was struggling with one of my first big assignments; in fact, I was feeling like I was carrying an impossible load of responsibility. In prayer, I complained to God about the situation. His answer to my worries came in a scripture a wonderful lady gave me soon thereafter, and what made this verse even more a "God thing" was that this saint had no idea what I was going through at the time.

She just approached me, obeying the Spirit's leading, and told me: "God has impressed me to share Lamentations 3:27 with you: 'It is good for a young man to bear the yoke while he is young.' I believe that God is using the things you are going through now to shape you for bigger things in the future."

Her words hit me hard. (Think of a dump truck unloading a few tons of bricks in your lap!) Once I was able to figuratively re-hinge my dropped jaw, I took that scripture to heart. Those same words have also helped me get through many tough times in the years since. Today, I am convinced that our struggles are God's tools to shape our lives and to prepare us for bigger responsibilities in His kingdom.

During a stint on a staff, I knew another officer who was both extremely talented and extremely ambitious. He was never content with the job he had; instead, he was constantly casting his vision toward the job he wanted next. The irony was, this obsessive focus on promotion kept him from the excellence in performance he could have achieved in his current post.

Eventually, it all caught up with him. His supervisor called him into his office and fired him. The superior was fed up with this officer's failure to devote his full attention to the task at hand because he had become so concentrated on the next step of the career ladder.

It's too bad this fellow didn't take to heart an axiom often repeated by military leaders: "The best job you will ever have is the one you have right now." In other words, if you perform your current responsibilities poorly, you will not be trusted in the future with bigger responsibilities.

This is true even when you feel you are stuck in a career rut, spinning your wheels, taking two steps back for every step forward...all those metaphors for job frustration you've ever heard. I have been there.

Once I found myself in what, at the time, seemed a no-win nightmare of a job. I had been warned by colleagues that this job would be a tough one, and that turned out to be a gross understatement. With the job came a jumble of perplexing personnel issues and technical challenges. In fact, when I had been on the job for just a few weeks, I had to brief a superior about why my organization had messed up one of his pet programs.

After a year and a half on that job, I felt like I had been parachuted into remotest Siberia and left to fend off bears and wolves with a pocketknife! Worse, I thought, was that I was just halfway through that three-year assignment. I resolved to grit my teeth and soldier on.

Then one night I received an urgent phone call from my supervisor. He had been informed that the superior who had called me on the carpet earlier wanted to see me again right away. Oh, boy. *So, what was wrong now?*

I was a bit apprehensive when I later walked into the superior's office, bracing for what was to come. However, instead of complaints, he told me to take a seat and then launched into a friendly, personal chat. I relaxed a bit, but in the back of my mind I was still wondering when the proverbial "other shoe" would drop.

Well, it never did. Instead, he said he had been watching me perform my current duties and wanted to help me get a promotion! Of course, I was shocked. He had two assignments in mind, both with wonderful responsibilities, and asked me to choose one of them.

I decided to return his trust by trusting him—and God through him—to choose. He wasted no time doing so, and then called some Air Force leaders to get the assignment rolling.

While I had felt banished to a tough, unrewarding job, I trusted the Lord and did what I knew He expected of me: to do the job I had in front of me, rather than lament over my situation to the point of helpless self-pity. God, as is His nature, used those difficulties I was facing—and an observant leader—to reward me.

Understand That Your Calling and Responsibilities Evolve and Grow as You Do Your Ordinary, Daily Tasks

Based on my own experience and watching how the lives of others unfold, I've come to the conclusion that growth never happens as fast as we would like it to. Here's what King Solomon once wrote about the concept:

A man's gift makes room for him, and brings him before great
men.

—PROVERBS 18:16

In ancient times, bringing a gift into an audience with royalty was
considered part of court protocol, a way of honoring the monarch and
earning his or her favor. But I believe the word *gift* in this passage
could just as well refer to the talents or God-given abilities of an individual. Gifts in this respect are honed and perfected over time.

For example, my public speaking has improved and become stronger
as I have exercised that ability. I am not the same public speaker I was
even five years ago. As I have allowed God to develop my speaking gift
and have dedicated it to bringing Him glory, God has opened doors
for me to speak in unexpected, previously untapped venues. This gift's
growth—from my initial, halting speaking abilities to the far more
confident and effective presentation I have today—took time. That talent's maturity came with being faithful where God gave opportunities and allowing the Lord to bring my public speaking seedling into
fuller bloom.

I often talk to people who are frustrated they do not have a larger
platform for their gifts to operate. In truth, God gives us as big a platform as He can trust us to use!

The Lord uses our ordinary, daily responsibilities to develop our talents, abilities, and our calling in life. Just as exercise develops strength
and stamina and boosts performance, God uses the day-to-day, seemingly mundane demands and challenges of our lives to build our character and gifts in readiness for that bigger arena of influence.

When we faithfully carry out our responsibilities within the various spheres of life (as husbands and wives, fathers and mothers, at
our current jobs, etc.), we really are progressing through the proving,
training, and growing that make up the ordinary, daily stuff of life.

In the Book of Acts, chapter 6, the Jerusalem church had a problem.
The good news was that they were reaching thousands with the Gospel.
The bad news was that they were not properly taking care of some
Gentile widows who were converts to Judaism and then Christianity.
So, the early church chose seven men—disciples known for their faith-
fulness and sterling characters—to oversee this ministry.

One of these men was Philip, who had a gift to share the message of Christ as an evangelist. Now he was being asked to wait tables. But Philip and the other six men not only were not offended by this new, humble assignment, they excelled at it!

> They presented these men to the apostles, who prayed and laid their hands on them.
>
> So the word of God spread. The number of disciples in Jerusalem increased rapidly, and a large number of priests became obedient to the faith.
>
> —Acts 6:6–7, niv

I believe that outsiders, seeing how the new sect lived up to its commitment to love and care for its most vulnerable members, were impressed by compassion in action and more open to listen to what Christ's followers had to say. Indeed, it seems like God found a way to use Philip's evangelistic gift even when it was expressed through serving tables!

Later, Philip was commissioned to carry the Gospel to the outcast Samaritans, an Ethiopian leader, and the important city of Caesarea (read about that in Acts 8). The point: Philip's gifts and calling evolved and grew as he performed those ordinary, daily tasks.

God Is Interested in How You Handle the So-Called Mundane, Menial, and Unimportant

This point of focus springs from our last discussion and expands on the idea of how God teaches us and prepares us for the big assignments by monitoring and correcting our progress in the small jobs. The Bible has much to teach on this concept:

> But David occasionally went and returned from Saul to feed his father's sheep at Bethlehem.
>
> And the Philistine drew near and presented himself forty days, morning and evening.
>
> Then Jesse said to his son David, "Take now for your brothers an ephah of this dried grain and these ten loaves, and run to your brothers at the camp. And carry these ten cheeses to the captain of their thousand, and see how your brothers fare, and bring back news of them."

> Now Saul and they and all the men of Israel were in the
> Valley of Elah, fighting with the Philistines. So David rose
> early in the morning, left the sheep with a keeper, and took
> the things and went as Jesse had commanded him. And he
> came to the camp as the army was going out to the fight and
> shouting for the battle.
>
> —1 SAMUEL 17:15–20

And these words from Jesus:

> "He who is faithful in what is least is faithful also in much;
> and he who is unjust in what is least is unjust also in much.
> Therefore if you have not been faithful in the unrighteous
> mammon, who will commit to your trust the true riches? And
> if you have not been faithful in what is another man's, who
> will give you what is your own?"
>
> —LUKE 16:10–12

Finally, what the Apostle Peter had to offer:

> Therefore humble yourselves under the mighty hand of God,
> that He may exalt you in due time, casting all your care upon
> Him, for He cares for you.
>
> —1 PETER 5:6–7

Do you see the thread that runs through each of these passages
and into the next? This is the theme: Our trustworthiness for bigger
responsibilities is proven in how we address those (to us) lackluster
and unimportant responsibilities in our lives!

Leaders, if you really want to know if you can trust someone with
bigger responsibilities, first watch how they handle a menial task you
give them. Assign that person a "dirty little job" that no one else wants
to do, and then watch how they carry out your assignment.

Do they show a good attitude? Are they diligent in their performance? Do they complain about their assignment to others or act like
their task is beneath them? Answers to those questions will tell you a
lot about others' faithfulness and determination to do their best work,

regardless of the assignment and if they can be trusted with bigger responsibilities.

Remember Luke 16:11 above: "Therefore if you have not been faithful in the unrighteous mammon, who will commit to your trust the true riches?"

Over my years as an officer, I had many opportunities to test staffers using these principles. If I wanted to find out if they were ready for a big job, I would assign them some menial task and then sit back and watch how they did it. They did not know that they were being tested, but I watched them very closely.

God tested David in the same way. The future king of Israel, the monarch God chose for favor and to begin a royal line that would culminate in Christ Himself, proved faithful in watching sheep and carrying food to his brothers on the front lines. That humble, trustworthy service opened the door for God to later use David as Israel's most successful military leader.

The simple truth: If a person doesn't do the small tasks well, that person cannot be trusted to perform bigger tasks, either.

BE A LIGHT FOR CHRIST IN ALL YOU DO

Earlier in this chapter, I shared how I had vowed at the beginning of my military career to integrate my Christian faith into all parts of my life. I am, first and foremost, an ambassador of Jesus Christ. This has not, however, meant that I figuratively jumped up on my soapbox and preached in my office. Certainly, I shared my faith when given the opportunity, but my bigger responsibility was to live a life that honored my Savior.

Jesus told us about the right attitude to have as His representatives:

> "You are the light of the world. A city that is set on a hill cannot be hidden. Nor do they light a lamp and put it under a basket, but on a lamp stand, and it gives light to all who are in the house. Let your light so shine before men, that they may see your good works and glorify your Father in heaven."
> —MATTHEW 5:14–16

You may be the only Christian light in your office, neighborhood, or sphere of influence. Be determined to let Christ shine through you!

Remember, people are watching you, especially if you are in a leadership position. They watch how you treat others, how you handle problems, how you deal with failure, and whether you live your life in accord with your stated principles.

Bottom line: You will either be a good witness for Christ or a bad one. There is no in-between category for godly leaders.

In one of my Air Force assignments, part of the job was to advise younger officers about their career development goals. It got so that, day to day, I would answer the same questions in telephone conversations over and over again. Some days, I would take as many as fifty such calls. Being only human, I was certainly tempted at times, upon hearing the same question yet again, to become impatient or to cut a conversation short.

In such moments, I silently prayed that instead God would shine through me to help me be a light to others. The Lord helped me realize that what seemed just another in a maddeningly long string of routine inquiries to me was a very important matter to the person on the other end of the line. The advice I was giving could actually make or break a career!

Well, God answered those prayers. Instead of regrets over possibly shortchanging someone, I was privileged to positively impact many of the lives of those who called me. I was able to do this with a timely kind word, some encouragement, occasionally some first direction—and best of all, taking the opportunity to verbally share my faith when God opened the door to do so.

Ironically, I recall another job where I had serious doubts that my Christian walk was affecting anyone. One day when I was feeling low about the effectiveness of my witness for Christ, I had a frank talk with my deputy who had recently accepted Jesus as his Savior.

"Does anyone notice a difference in my life?" I asked. His answer surprised and encouraged me. He told me that not only did people notice how my faith directed my life and interactions with them, but my example was frequently the topic of conversation by my subordinates.

So, I learned that even when we feel like our quiet testimony is stillborn, it is not. People are watching. Whether we feel like it or not, our faithfulness to Christ will impact the lives of those around us.

I challenge you as a Christian leader to let the Lord shine through you. First, be a witness for Christ by how you live your life. And if you have the opportunity, share your faith in conversation. But never underestimate the power of living your faith and principles!

St. Francis of Assisi put it this way: "Preach the Gospel at all times, and when necessary, use words."

Reflections

- Lord, nothing is "secular" in my life; everything has a spiritual component.

- I will give You my best in all I do.

- I will do everything as if You are watching me.

- Forgive me, Lord, for thinking some jobs, callings, or responsibilities are more important than others.

- You are shaping me for future responsibilities through the daily responsibilities I have right now.

- I understand that my gifts and calling will grow over time.

- Forgive me for always wanting things to happen in a revolutionary way.

- The gifts you have given will grow and open doors.

- God, I want to do a much better job in handling the mundane, the menial, and the things I thought unimportant.

- Forgive me for murmuring a lot in the past.

- These things are Your yardstick to measure my faithfulness for bigger things.

- Whatever I do, Lord, I want to be light for You. Shine through me, Jesus, in all I say or do!

Chapter Nine

THE INADEQUACY OF THE LEADER

I F ANYONE KNEW about being propelled unprepared into massive responsibilities, it had to be Harry S. Truman.

The son of a Missouri farmer, he struggled to rise from simple, rural roots. His big chance to make something of himself came with America's entry into World War I, and even that required him to secretly memorize the eye test chart in order to trick Army doctors into passing him for enlistment. (Even with spectacles, his eyesight was substandard.) He ended up an artillery officer of modest accomplishments, and after the war, his stint as a storekeeper ended in bankruptcy.

Then things began to turn around. Truman entered politics with the help of his influential in-laws, initially as a judge and then as a senatorial candidate who rode the Depression-era Democratic Party wave into office.

In 1944, President Franklin D. Roosevelt reluctantly chose Truman as a running mate; the Missourian was considered to afford Roosevelt the best chance of not offending any of the special interest groups plaguing a nation weary of World War II. Once elected to his fourth term, however, Roosevelt left his new vice president out of the decision-making entirely.

Then, on April 12, 1944, less than three months after his election, Roosevelt died. Suddenly, Truman, the political compromise, was sworn in as president. He was, at least at first, as bewildered a chief executive as the United States likely had ever seen.

After taking the oath of office, a humbled and overwhelmed Truman turned to journalists covering the event and lamented, "Boys, if you ever pray, pray for me now. I don't know if you fellas ever had a load of hay fall on you, but when they told me what happened yesterday, I felt like the moon, the stars, and all the planets had fallen on me."

111

Would you expect this man, flooded by feelings of inadequacy as he was thrust unprepared into leadership of the Free World, to find the grit and wisdom needed to finally bring victory over the Nazis in Europe and Japanese in the Pacific? History records that he did. Perhaps those prayers he asked for had a lot to do with that.

The Bible tells us about another leader, Moses, who started out nearly crippled by self-doubt. Moses even argued with God about the wisdom of choosing him to bring the Israelites out of Egyptian slavery:

> Moses said to the Lord, "O my Lord, I am not eloquent, neither before nor since You have spoken to Your servant, but I am slow of speech and slow of tongue."
>
> —Exodus 4:10

Not a promising start for the man who would later be revered as the greatest of the prophets, a leader accompanied by miracles and entrusted to deliver an everlasting covenant between God and a new nation, sealed with the Ten Commandments.

But the Lord seems to relish turning the uncertain, frightened, and inadequate into heroes of faith and godly leaders of renown! How? Consider these familiar scriptural passages in a fresh light:

> Surely he took up our infirmities and carried our sorrows, yet we considered him stricken by God, smitten by him, and afflicted. But he was pierced for our transgressions, he was crushed for our iniquities; the punishment that brought us peace was upon him, and by his wounds we are healed.
>
> —Isaiah 53:4–5, niv

> When evening came, many who were demon-possessed were brought to him, and he drove out the spirits with a word and healed all the sick. This was to fulfill what was spoken through the prophet Isaiah: "He took up our infirmities and carried our diseases."
>
> —Matthew 8:16–17, niv

Of course, the most obvious promise contained in these verses is for God's healing in our bodies. But look a bit deeper, and you can see the Lord's provision, wonderful as it is, goes far beyond the obvious.

He heals our diseases, yes, but He also bore our infirmities as He was lifted up on the cross. The word *infirmities* in Isaiah 53:4–5 and Matthew 8:16–17 has a dual meaning. It means sickness, but it can also be translated "anxiety or inadequacy" (also see 2 Corinthians 12:10).

In other words, we each face situations every day that are beyond our abilities. We are unable to fix, repair, improve, or heal a situation or perform a task up to others' expectations.

This battle with our infirmities or feelings of inadequacy is common to us all. We all feel inadequate, overwhelmed, or helpless at one time or another, and those feelings lead to shame and isolation. And admit it: We feel like we are the only one struggling with such feelings and often are reluctant to share them with anyone else.

Here's how the Bible explains this phenomenon:

> No test or temptation that comes your way is beyond the course of what others have had to face. All you need to remember is that God will never let you down; he'll never let you be pushed past your limit; he'll always be there to help you come through it.
>
> —1 Corinthians 10:13, the message

We can and should share our infirmities and inadequacies with God. And knowing that the Lord often counsels us through the words of wise brothers and sisters in the faith, we should not be afraid to share these feelings with a trusted brother or sister, either.

We all scrap and claw on the same battlefields, fighting the temptations to sin in word, thought, or deed. Our tests in life, along with the debilitating doubts and emotions that often come with them, also are all too common. I know that at times when I've shared a particular struggle with a trusted counselor, I often am surprised to learn they are struggling in the same area.

Instead of talking about our challenges and praying for answers with these trusted others, don't we all too often bottle these issues up inside and seek a temporary escape? Think about it: When is the last time you turned to television, alcohol, sweets, or junk food as you "self-medicated" a troubled soul?

Here's another troubling truth: Feelings of inadequacy grow as your leadership responsibilities increase. It all makes sense if you think about it. Bigger responsibilities mean bigger challenges. Still, we need to learn how to not let those feelings paralyze us into helpless inaction.

I have found that when I feel those waves of inadequacy beginning to roll in, there is great help in the Scriptures and in sharing with trusted, mature leaders. Here are some verses I especially treasure for such times, followed by some principles for dealing with those challenges when we just don't feel up to what God has called us to do:

> For it is God who works in you both to will and to do for His good pleasure.
>
> —Philippians 2:13

> I can do all things through Christ who strengthens me.
>
> —Philippians 4:13

> For you see your calling, brethren, that not many wise according to the flesh, not many mighty, not many noble, are called. But God has chosen the foolish things of the world to put to shame the wise, and God has chosen the weak things of the world to put to shame the things which are mighty; and the base things of the world and the things which are despised God has chosen, and the things which are not, to bring to nothing the things that are, that no flesh should glory in His presence. But of Him you are in Christ Jesus, who became for us wisdom from God—and righteousness and sanctification and redemption—that, as it is written, "He who glories, let him glory in the Lord."
>
> —1 Corinthians 1:26–31

> And He said to me, "My grace is sufficient for you, for My strength is made perfect in weakness." Therefore most gladly I will rather boast in my infirmities, that the power of Christ may rest upon me. Therefore I take pleasure in infirmities, in

reproaches, in needs, in persecutions, in distresses, for Christ's sake. For when I am weak, then I am strong.

—2 CORINTHIANS 12:9–10

So Jesus answered and said to them, "Have faith in God. For assuredly, I say to you, whoever says to this mountain, 'Be removed and be cast into the sea,' and does not doubt in his heart, but believes that those things he says will be done, he will have whatever he says. Therefore I say to you, whatever things you ask when you pray, believe that you receive them, and you will have them."

—MARK 11:22–24

And finally, this passage (I will show later in this chapter why I also include these verses):

Then it happened, as they continued on and talked, that suddenly a chariot of fire appeared with horses of fire, and separated the two of them; and Elijah went up by a whirlwind into heaven.

And Elisha saw it, and he cried out, "My father, my father, the chariot of Israel and its horsemen!" So he saw him no more. And he took hold of his own clothes and tore them into two pieces. He also took up the mantle of Elijah that had fallen from him, and went back and stood by the bank of the Jordan.

—2 KINGS 2:11–13

EIGHT PRINCIPLES FOR DEALING WITH FEELINGS OF INADEQUACY

1. God has chosen the weak to accomplish great things.

The Apostle Paul made this abundantly clear in his writings to the ancient church:

But God has chosen the foolish things of the world to put to shame the wise, and God has chosen the weak things of the world to put to shame the things which are mighty; and the base things of the world and the things which are despised

God has chosen, and the things which are not, to bring to nothing the things that are, that no flesh should glory in His presence.

—1 Corinthians 1:27–29

When God gives you a task, it will always be bigger than what you can do on your own. That is because our heavenly Father loves to demonstrate His power to the world by doing extraordinary things through ordinary people and humble leaders.

So, we certainly have nothing to lose by being honest with ourselves and with God (who knows all about them, anyway) when it comes to our weaknesses and inadequacies. The key is going a step beyond that, though, by confessing that His power is glorified through our weaknesses. The Bible is full of stories about God doing impossible things through men and women who let Him use them.

2. Understand that when God truly leads you to do something, He will supply the needed resources.

For it is God who works in you both to will and to do for His good pleasure.

—Philippians 2:13

That's Brother Paul again, making it clear that God will not only give us the inspiration to do a task, but He also will empower us to do it. In other words, the Lord will give you His supernatural strength, His wisdom, His finances, the people you need to help you, and anything else you need! When we worry about the resources we need to do something God has called us to, we are taking on a responsibility God reserves to Himself. He promised to give us the resources we need, so quit worrying.

3. The resources you need will be there when you need them, not before!

That is just the way God works, and it is a principle that is vitally important to grasp. Sure, it flies in the face of human logic, but God is *God.* He is the master of time and timing and knows perfectly when provision, open doors, encouragement, and all the other things that go into success are needed by His servants to fulfill His callings.

Our worrying and impatience will not rush Him. His plans for us will unfold in *His* time. Still, we can rest assured in His promises to always be on time with what we need, when we need it:

> And my God will meet all your needs according to his glorious riches in Christ Jesus.
> —Philippians 4:19, NIV

It is vital that, as Christian leaders, we grasp this two-pronged concept of God's provision and His timing. If we can do that, He will teach us not only to move toward an unwavering trust in Him, but we will also be enlightened as to how He works and how we can walk more resolutely and effectively in His ways.

4. Don't look too far into the future; you will feel overwhelmed if you do.

There is nothing like riding a wild horse called *Imagination* toward the twin peaks of *Anxiety* and *Fear* for making any leader feel even more inadequate. That makes perfect sense, too, because when you look too far down that trail of speculation, you also put yourself ahead of God's resources.

So instead of putting the spurs to that particular steed of the mind, remember: *His resources arrive when needed, not before!* God is faithful to provide the mental, emotional, spiritual, and physical blessings needed for today's tasks. Tomorrow's resources will be there *tomorrow*.

Jesus put it this way:

> "So don't worry about tomorrow, for tomorrow will bring its own worries. Today's trouble is enough for today."
> —Matthew 6:34, NLT

5. God's grace is like a coat; when the task is done, He removes it.

Think of God's grace as being like a coat. A coat serves a variety of purposes, from protecting its wearer from the elements to warding off cold; as a designation of authority, such as a military or police officer's uniform; or for a specific purpose or event, like a tuxedo you may wear to a wedding or an elegant social occasion. When its purpose is fulfilled, the coat is removed.

The Old Testament prophet Elijah wore a cloak (the ancient Middle East's coat) that was a symbol of his spiritual authority. The time came, though, when God removed Elijah's cloak. In 2 Kings 2:11–14, we learn the story of Elijah's final hours, with his prophetic protégé, Elisha, following him to soak up every bit of wisdom and blessing he could in preparation for being Elijah's successor.

Elisha was there when God took Elijah, watching the prophet's cloak fall to the ground as he was lifted up to heaven. Elijah's cloak is a wonderful picture of God's grace. When the prophet's earthly work was complete, this mantle of God was lifted from his life and passed on to Elisha.

Three decades of service in the Armed Forces repeatedly took me through tough times when I felt a portion of God's grace lifting from my life, only to be replaced by His blessings for a new leadership role. In fact, I could often tell when a change in responsibilities was about to happen (even before anyone told me) by this feeling that a particular mantle of grace was lifting from me.

Those times can be both exciting and scary. As God tugs that old, familiar cloak from your shoulders, you feel a bit naked to the overwhelming world of challenges out there. Then He wraps you in a new garment of grace—one you can sense is better crafted to see you through the next assignment in life. Be aware of these spiritual transitions, and you will better handle change when it comes.

6. Don't compare yourself to someone else; their coat is different from yours.

When it comes to donning that coat of grace God provides His leaders, forget about that being a "one size fits all" proposition. Different callings, different responsibilities, different giftings... *different people.* For each one of us, God's resources and grace are custom-made!

So, don't look at where God has placed you or what He is calling on you to accomplish and compare yourself to others. Going down that road is not only as senseless as making the proverbial comparison of apples to oranges, but it is a recipe for frustration and heightened feelings of inadequacy.

Consider what God's Word says about this:

For we dare not class ourselves or compare ourselves with those who commend themselves. But they, measuring themselves by themselves, and comparing themselves among themselves, are not wise. We, however, will not boast beyond measure, but within the limits of the sphere which God appointed us — a sphere which especially includes you.

—2 Corinthians 10:12–13

Paul gives very clear instruction in this passage:

- God gives each leader boundaries of responsibility.

- Unwise leaders compare themselves to others.

- Other leaders are not your benchmark; you are not to measure your worth by watching another leader.

- Focus on what God has told you to do, and rejoice when you accomplish it.

7. If God gives you great abilities in an area, expect Him to test you in that area.

If you have ever watched a talented athlete—a professional football, basketball, or baseball star in his prime—you probably have thought or heard a television sports commentator declare, "He makes it look so easy!"

Of course, it isn't easy at all. Just try to duplicate that one-handed touchdown catch, that game-winning 3-point basket as time runs out, or that World Series–clinching home run with thousands, perhaps millions of fans screaming their lungs out! No, such high-level performances require the kind of skill and confidence that only comes with seemingly endless hours of practice, hard work, repeated failures, teamwork, correction from coaches, stints on the bench, and focus on the task when the world around you swirls in chaos and emotion.

God also hones our talents and abilities. He uses other people, setbacks, various experiences, and many other things to bring us to our spiritual peak of performance *in Him*. Yes, God wants us to learn to rely on Him and not our own abilities. When we give those abilities back to God, then and only then can they be used in truly powerful ministry to others.

In fact, without God's blessing, empowerment, and direction, we will always see our best efforts in ministerial leadership eventually unravel, and likely much sooner than later. But when our talents and focus are given wholly over to the Lord, our service to the kingdom will have an impact far beyond human abilities or human imaginations.

8. Learn the difficult lesson now: it is not about you; it is all about God.

At the root of inadequacy is the always-fatal flaw of self-focus. Looking in a mirror gives you a complete view of you, but if you try to hike up a rugged mountain trail with a mirror held in front of your face, expect to stumble and fall—perhaps a very long way! If our eyes are only on ourselves, we cannot see God's direction, provision, or plan.

Focusing on ourselves keeps us from trying new things, from believing God could use us, and from trusting God for supernatural results. Next up on that road is a dismal room at Motel Inadequacy, and before you know it, that room morphs into a spiritually debilitating prison cell.

Focusing on ourselves produces fear and despair. But if you shift your focus to God, you can experience the freeing power of faith. The Bible has much to say about that principle:

> "O our God, will you not judge them? For we have no power to face this vast army that is attacking us. We do not know what to do, but our eyes are upon you."
> —2 Chronicles 20:12, niv

Reflections

- Have you let feelings of inadequacy rule you as a leader? Remember that Jesus made provision for your infirmities or feelings of inadequacy on the cross.

- Which of the eight principles helped you the most?

- What do you need to do right now to implement what you have learned?

- Would it be helpful to carry a card with Scripture passages relating to feelings of inadequacy?

Please pause and pray the following:

Lord, please forgive me for letting my feelings of inadequacy rule me. I did not understand that everyone else feels the same way. I now see that You want to teach me to trust in You. Feeling inadequate is normal when I walk with You. I want to learn to trust You and not my abilities. I am excited that when You give me a task, it is always bigger than me. I cannot do it without Your resources.

I thank You that those resources arrive just when I need them. Thank You for the desire, wisdom, strength, and people I need to do what You call me to do. Bring glory to Your name through what You do in and through me. In Jesus' name I pray, Amen.

Chapter Ten

THE INSECURITY OF THE LEADER

ARLIER IN THIS book, I briefly touched on the biblical story of Gideon, that reluctant military leader God used to bring about a victory over an army of oppressors with what was comparatively just a handful of warriors. I want to return to Gideon now as we explore the challenge of overcoming insecurity and building our faith and trust in God's provision for all our leadership needs.

I am greatly indebted to Gwyn Vaughn, a pastor and leader in our association of churches (Grace International Churches and Ministries). At our national convention in 2004, his message about Gideon greatly impressed me, and it will now provide the foundation for what I am about to share with you.

In chapter 9, we explored that crippling sense of inadequacy most leaders feel at one time or another. Now we will take the wraps off inadequacy's twin brother, insecurity. And these brothers, while not identical, certainly seem close; you will almost always find them walking tentatively through your mind and spirit, hand in hand.

Let's look at some key scriptures that relate to Gideon's battle with insecurity:

> Then the children of Israel did evil in the sight of the LORD. So the LORD delivered them into the hand of Midian for seven years, and the hand of Midian prevailed against Israel. Because of the Midianites, the children of Israel made for themselves the dens, the caves, and the strongholds which are in the mountains. So it was, whenever Israel had sown, Midianites would come up; also Amalekites and the people of the East would come up against them. Then they would encamp against them and destroy the produce of the earth as far as Gaza, and leave no sustenance for Israel, neither sheep

nor ox nor donkey. For they would come up with their live-stock and their tents, coming in as numerous as locusts; both they and their camels were without number; and they would enter the land to destroy it. So Israel was greatly impoverished because of the Midianites, and the children of Israel cried out to the LORD.

—JUDGES 6:1–6

Now the Angel of the LORD came and sat under the tere-binth tree which was in Ophrah, which belonged to Joash the Abiezrite, while his son Gideon threshed wheat in the wine press, in order to hide it from the Midianites. And the Angel of the LORD appeared to him, and said to him, "The LORD is with you, you mighty man of valor!"

Gideon said to Him, "O my lord, if the LORD is with us, why then has all this happened to us? And where are all His miracles which our fathers told us about, saying, 'Did not the LORD bring us up from Egypt?' But now the Lord has for-saken us and delivered us into the hands of the Midianites."

Then the LORD turned to him and said, "Go in this might of yours, and you shall save Israel from the hand of the Midianites. Have I not sent you?"

—JUDGES 6:11–14

And this from Paul:

For you see your calling, brethren, that not many wise according to the flesh, not many mighty, not many noble, are called. But God has chosen the foolish things of the world to put to shame the wise, and God has chosen the weak things of the world to put to shame the things which are mighty; and the base things of the world and the things which are despised God has chosen, and the things which are not, to bring to nothing the things that are, that no flesh should glory in His presence.

—1 CORINTHIANS 1:26–29

God's Word is packed with stories about men and women He called upon to do something *big*—something outside their comfort zones, beyond their pay grade, or whatever other metaphor you want to use for *just plain beyond their natural abilities*. Time and time again, God chose unlikely heroes to be vessels for His spirit and power.

These men and women of faith didn't know where to start. They struggled with personal issues that threatened to derail their commitment to the mission. They felt totally inadequate for the task. And they asked the same question: "Why me?"

What unites all of them? As you read through Scripture, you cannot help but notice that the people God uses have one thing in common: They were ordinary people. Very few of them were influential, came from the upper crust of society, or were highly trained in what God was asking them to do. In fact, most Bible characters struggled with crippling personal challenges as God asked these ordinary servants to do extraordinary things for the kingdom.

Yes, these reluctant heroes of the faith never began believing that God might use them to help others who faced a desperate situation. They usually waited until God forcibly drafted them because they believed others certainly could do a better job. What they could not—would not—see was that God had *already* chosen the best candidates for the job...*them*.

Time for some personal honesty here, dear reader. We all struggle to some degree with feelings of insecurity. What stirs your insecurity juices to the point of miserable spiritual heartburn? Is it speaking in front of people, having to organize and lead a group, a lack of education, or maybe an underestimation of your talents, however latent they may be?

That earlier passage from St. Paul (1 Cor. 1:26–29) drives home a humbling and powerful point: God most often uses ordinary people to do His work. At first, that just doesn't seem logical, does it? But think about the Lord's nature and consider, and you will see there are actually a couple of obvious and sensible reasons for God's formula for leadership success in this instance.

First, ordinary people know that they will have to trust in God if something is to happen. Second, ordinary folks are less likely to take the credit when something does happen.

Gideon was an ordinary person called by God to do a big task.

Remember, when the angel of the Lord appeared to him and declared him to be a big-shot military genius, Gideon was hiding from the Midianite enemy, afraid of his own shadow! Yet God chose this ordinary, scared little rabbit of a man and transformed him into a warrior who would lead the army of Israel to an improbable (outside of the Lord's blessing) victory.

Here are six lessons we can learn from Gideon, the insecure leader.

We Need to Learn How to Discern God's Voice

The Scriptures give us some good detail about the first time God spoke to Gideon. It was not an auspicious start for our hero. Back in Judges 6:11–13 for a moment, we find Gideon in his hideout, the wine press, threshing wheat out of sight of the Midianite oppressors. Boom! The Angel of the Lord is suddenly there, and he bellows, "The Lord is with you, you mighty man of valor!" I can almost see Gideon jumping out of his sandals, maybe even trying to shush his visitor—surely the Midianites would hear! But Gideon instead gulps and, shall we say, expresses his doubts. Obviously, he must think, this angel has the wrong address!

Gideon continued, "If the Lord is with us, why then has all this happened to us? And where are the miracles which our fathers told us about.... The Lord has forsaken us and delivered us into the hands of the Midianites."

Almost immediately, a big mental "oops" must have echoed in Gideon's mind. Judges 6:22 has our hero, as the full import of his angelic visit slaps him across the skull like a thunderbolt, reeling with an impending sense of doom: "Now Gideon perceived that He was the Angel of the Lord. So Gideon said, 'Alas, O Lord God! For I have seen the Angel of the Lord face to face.'"

Did you notice that Gideon was a bit slow on the uptake here, that he didn't seem to realize he was talking to an angel? OK, laugh if you must, but it's not that Gideon was as dumb as the ox he probably was using to grind out flour from that wheat he was threshing. *Gideon was not that different from you or me.* There is a learning process to discerning God's voice from the multitude of competing voices or just plain noise that comprises our consciousness.

Gideon was sent an angel to demand his attention, and even then, it took a while. More often, God speaks to us through the natural conduits of life rather than supernatural manifestations. He can speak to our hearts just as clearly as that angel through prayerful examination of Scripture. Read the Bible and thoughtfully apply it to your own life, your own current challenges, your future hopes, and, yes, even your fears.

God may speak to you through a picture in your mind, or it may be through words of wisdom from others who just seem to have *that something* of truth about them that you feel deep inside. Or He may speak through a gentle impression as you pray or study His Word.

In the opening chapter of Paul's epistle to the Hebrews, the apostle tells us that God strives to get our attention in many ways, and He yearns to speak to us directly through the life and living testimony of His Son, Jesus:

> God, who at various times and in various ways spoke in time past to the fathers by the prophets, has in these last days spoken to us by His Son, whom He has appointed heir of all things, through whom also He made the worlds.
>
> —HEBREWS 1:1–2

How many times do we dismiss God's voice because we mistake it for our own thoughts? When we are fighting the flood that is the cacophony of life—or just because of our own insecurity—that dismissal of the divine voice can easily occur. Still, I am convinced that the Lord wants to speak to each of us. Evidence that He is speaking may be confirmed as you feel that rush of a new sense of purpose, excitement mixed with fear, and new vision.

Act on those gentle impressions from the Father, and it will become easier to confidently recognize His voice in the future. Remember, it's a learning process.

As I readied for one of my first excursions to a foreign country as a minister, I remember telling God that I would do anything He asked me to do. God took me at my word and asked me to do an altar call (asking people to come forward to accept Christ publicly) as I was walking up to the podium to deliver my first message.

Despite my promise to do anything He asked, I balked. "God, I haven't even spoken yet. I have never been with this group before. Lord, this doesn't make sense to me." This conversation within my thoughts and spirit seemed to go on and on, until finally what had started as a gentle impression became more insistent. Hadn't I vowed I would do anything the Lord asked?

Busted.

So, I mentally gulped, a little surprised but grimly determined to keep my word. Even my interpreter was surprised when I asked him to tell the audience that I was not going to share a message! Instead, I told them God was dealing with a number of them about sin and disobedience in their lives. I shared a few more thoughts along that line and then invited any who felt God's conviction to come forward.

Much to my dismay, no one made a move for what seemed like an eternity. Then, finally, a young woman stood up and started forward. Her courage broke the dam, and almost all the people broke into tears and sobs and then joined her. The Lord reconciled many to Him that night—and taught a rather contrite retired-Air-Force-officer-turned-minister a lesson about better discerning the voice of his Master!

It was the lesson of Gideon, with a twist, perhaps, but still the basic, age-old call to trust and act on God's word. The more we move ahead with what the Lord tells us, the easier it is to hear and obey in the future.

You Must Overcome the Doubts About Whether God Can Use Us or Not

God spoke through the angel to tell Gideon that he was to lead the army of Israel in victory over the Midianites. Does the tone of this initial response from this "mighty man of valor" echo anywhere, perhaps in your memories?

> Then the LORD turned to him and said, "Go in this might of yours, and you shall save Israel from the hand of the Midianites. Have I not sent you?"
>
> So he said to Him, "O my LORD, how can I save Israel? Indeed my clan is the weakest in Manasseh, and I am the least in my father's house."

> And the LORD said to him, "Surely I will be with you, and you shall defeat the Midianites as one man."
>
> —JUDGES 6:14–16

Gideon did not believe God could use him. He gave in to his lurking insecurity and let those feelings overcome what an angel was telling him! That's how powerful self-doubt—and in this case, *God-doubt*—can be, even in the presence of the Almighty. How many times have you and I been a "Gideon"?

God told Gideon the secret to success would be "I will be with you." And He has the same unbreakable, eternal promise for His leaders today. Write it down. It is an equation as true as Einstein's famous $E=MC^2$: *God's presence is the key to success.*

It is not our confidence, our abilities, our wisdom, or even our past victories. It is all about God. He wants to use each of us. The question is, will we let Him?

When I was in my twenties, God healed me from a skin condition through someone's prayers. Later, I remember saying to myself, "I wish God would use me to pray for healing in others." That opportunity came on many future occasions, but I remember one situation in particular.

On one of my trips to Honduras, I spoke in a church about praying for healing, sharing numerous scriptures. I also shared about my own personal experiences of healing prayers answered by the Lord—and in concluding my message, I joined local church leaders in praying for those who came forward.

The first man responding to the invitation was in a wheelchair, and I asked him to attempt to stand with my assistance. Grabbing his arms, I helped him take some steps. As he started moving, I prayed aloud that God would strengthen his legs and help him walk. I did not see much improvement in his mobility. Quite frankly, I was disappointed that more visible healing had not occurred in this man. After a few minutes, I helped him back to his wheelchair and proceeded to pray for others who had come forward.

Later that evening, the local pastor surprised me—and considerably uplifted my spirit—when he told me that the man in the wheelchair had previously been unable to move his legs at all; that he had been able to take even halting steps amazed the pastor and congregation alike.

Lesson: I did not have to personally witness God's healing power to be a catalyst for it. My responsibility was to simply be obedient and pray. Like He always does, God takes our offerings—whether sacrifices of money, time, or the spirit—and multiplies them in astounding ways!

You Have to Tear Down Altars That Appear to Be Sacred but Offend God

One of the first things God told Gideon to do was to tear down the family altar. Try this today, and you would be angrily castigated for being intolerant or religiously bigoted. But truth is uncompromising; it was some three thousand years ago, and it is today. God is God; there is no other:

> Now it came to pass the same night that the LORD said to him, "Take your father's young bull, the second bull of seven years old, and tear down the altar of Baal that your father has, and cut down the wooden image that is beside it; and build an altar to the LORD your God on top of this rock in the proper arrangement, and take the second bull and offer a burnt sacrifice with the wood of the image which you shall cut down."
> —JUDGES 6:25–26

Then, an altar was seen as the means of reaching out to the divine. Today, we don't pile up rocks, slaughter animals, and burn them, but we have our metaphorical altars nonetheless. We rely on rituals created by men, rote prayers, maybe even "name it and claim it," God-as-a-cosmic-Santa-Claus incantations to connect with the Lord (or, perhaps, we think, bend God to our wants?).

Whatever form our modern altars take, we are relying on things to reach God that are offensive to Him or just don't work. These altars have to be torn down if we want God to use us!

In Gideon's case, that altar belonged to his father. His family had gone through tough times and decided that a pagan altar might be the answer to their problems. Maybe Gideon's father thought he was just covering all his supernatural bases. Regardless, that altar led this family further away from God, not toward Him.

In the patriarchal societies of the ancient Middle East, going against one's father was not only frowned upon, but it could also bring banishment or even death. So, destroying his father's shrine was a serious infraction, not just what today would be misdemeanor vandalism. Still, Gideon finally trusted God and had determined to obey Him, believing the Lord to handle the consequences. (Gideon's dad, Joash, actually defended his son when the mob demanded the offender's life for this "crime.")

Today, too, we often have to destroy "altars" of family tradition or religious customs when God shows us they are not grounded in Scripture. Tearing them down, whether that amounts to shedding preconceptions about how God can or will work through us or acting on His direction when it comes through unaccustomed channels or means, is essential to growth toward effective and blessed leadership.

I once had to tear down an altar of my own making, one that had me convinced that whether I had God's love and approval was directly tied to my efforts to please Him. This was the furthest thing from the truth, and to believe otherwise denied that God had long ago showed His unconditional love by sending His Son to die on a cross for my sins. Nothing I could do could make Him love me more.

I asked God to tear down this altar in my life and to forgive me for trying to earn His approval. Freed of the spiritually crippling demands of that altar, I discovered God's unmerited love is liberating.

What altars do *you* need to tear down?

YOU MUST LEARN TO WORK WITH PEOPLE DIFFERENT FROM YOU

One of the under-appreciated miracles of how God works is the way He brings people of vastly different backgrounds, intellect, skill, and ethnicity together to move His kingdom forward. Think of Gideon: He had to work with an oppressed, discouraged, and fractured Israel to accomplish his mission, a nation divided along its twelve tribal lines and territory, and each of those clans beset by petty leaders with their own jealous egos.

Here's one example:

> Now the Ephraimites asked Gideon, "Why have you treated
> us like this? Why didn't you call us when you wanted to fight
> Midian?" And they criticized him sharply.
>
> —JUDGES 8:1, NIV

Gideon had been given a mission by God to lead an Israeli army
against Midian. But getting that army together was like trying to herd
cats! It seemed like everyone had an opinion on how things needed
to be done, and even after Gideon's miraculous success in routing
the massively larger Midianite forces, the bruised egos whined and
complained and blistered with ill-concealed envy and frustrated
self-promotion.

What happens to you when you are forced to work with people
different from you? Are you intimidated by the differences? Do you
become angry when they don't think like you? Do you want to quit
when they criticize you?

Like it or not (and I suggest you might as well learn to like it!), we
will always have to work with people different from us. God made
us as individuals who need to learn to work together to accomplish
almost everything in life that matters, and especially as leaders in His
service. Further, God brings balance to our lives through interaction
and acceptance (however grudging) of those "different" others.

Personal and spiritual growth can be painful, just like physical
growth from childhood into maturity, when there are times when our
bones and muscles ache with the stretching of growth. A wonderful
thing happens after the growth and discomfort, though. We become
stronger.

Stretching also improves flexibility and, subsequently, ability and
performance. Any athlete can tell you that. It is why, in any sport you
can think of, a pre-competition period of stretching is routine. The
same principle applies to spiritual growth and preparation for the
challenges ahead.

Interaction with different co-workers and subordinates also provides the canvas upon which God can paint direction and correction
for you. We simply are not made to do it all ourselves. We need each
other in everyday life, and God's kingdom model for us is to blend
our widely varied gifts, personalities, resources, and callings together
within the body of Christ.

Being members in that spiritual body under God's love not only helps us to accomplish miracles together, but that body of Christ also makes each one of us the best we can be, if we allow the Holy Spirit to work in and through us:

> For in fact the body is not one member but many.
>
> —1 CORINTHIANS 12:14

> But now indeed there are many members, yet one body. And the eye cannot say to the hand, "I have no need of you"; nor again the head to the feet, "I have no need of you."
>
> —1 CORINTHIANS 12:20–21

> And He Himself gave some to be apostles, some prophets, some evangelists, and some pastors and teachers, for the equipping of the saints for the work of ministry, for the edifying of the body of Christ, till we all come to the unity of the faith and of the knowledge of the Son of God, to a perfect man, to the measure of the stature of the fullness of Christ; that we should no longer be children, tossed to and fro and carried about with every wind of doctrine, by the trickery of men, in the cunning craftiness of deceitful plotting, but, speaking the truth in love, may grow up in all things into Him who is the head—Christ—from whom the whole body, joined and knit together by what every joint supplies, according to the effective working by which every part does its share, causes growth of the body for the edifying of itself in love.
>
> —EPHESIANS 4:11–16

YOU MUST LEARN TO FOLLOW ORDERS IF YOU WANT TO GIVE THEM

Now, be honest. If you had been Gideon and God told you, "Hey, I want you to take three hundred guys and attack that huge Midianite army. Don't worry; I'll be with you," wouldn't you think, *Wait a minute. This just doesn't make any sense!*

Now, step into the present. Think of your own peculiar experiences where you felt led of the Lord to take a seemingly nonsensical step. How did you handle that? Did you balk, or did you grit your teeth and leap, trusting (well, hoping) God would truly grab you by the hand? Conversely, have you had a boss give you directions that seemed, at first, just plain dumb?

While you mull over those questions, let's revisit the orders God gave to Gideon about trimming the size of his army:

> And the LORD said to Gideon, "The people who are with you are too many for Me to give the Midianites into their hands, lest Israel claim glory for itself against Me, saying, 'My own hand has saved me.'"
>
> —JUDGES 7:2

It had been hard work for Gideon to convince the oppressed Israelites to flock to his banner, but thirty-two thousand of them had done so. But now God was telling Gideon that this army—a fraction the size of their opponents—was too large! Gideon must have been flabbergasted.

That sense of trepidation must have only grown deeper as God proceeded to whittle down the host—first to ten thousand men, and then to just three hundred. God wasn't through, however; next, the Lord told Gideon they would be using lanterns and trumpets as their primary weapons.

Wow. Would you follow these orders?

Gideon and his few men did follow those orders. Vastly outnumbered, they had no choice but to trust God for the victory...or turn tail and run back to their wine-press hiding places. The Bible recounts what happened next: Gideon and his lantern-busting, trumpet-blowing band came screaming out of the hills, and the Midianite army started fighting...itself. The Midianite horde that the Bible describes as "without number, as the sand of the seashore in multitude" broke into a rout.

God had won this battle. Gideon and his band, now joined by other Israelites, had nothing to do but the cleanup, chasing and killing the panic-stricken Midianites by the tens of thousands and lifting the oppressors' chokehold on the nation of Israel.

Rather straightforward, isn't it? God can choose any method He wants. If you want a formula to follow, forget it. There is no figuring out the Lord's stratagems, and the Bible is replete with such seemingly strange orders from God. The only safe, wise thing to do is to obey what the Lord tells you to do. This is the most important lesson any Christian leader can learn.

In fact, God will not trust you to lead others unless you have first learned to follow His orders.

There was a time in my early Christian walk when God told me that I was to "sit for a year." Eventually, I understood that what He wanted me to do with that respite was to spend time in His presence, praying, studying, and growing inwardly.

You see, at that point in my life, I had become too prone to believing spiritual growth only came with activity; I had to be doing for God, rather than allowing the Lord to do for me—to mold my perceptions, understanding, and maturity as I took the time to learn and listen to His voice.

That year was a tremendous time of learning, re-prioritizing, and maturing for me. I discovered I had run way ahead of my wife in a ministry God meant for us to share. Instead, a walk that we had begun together had changed into a one-man race of activity. I finally noticed that she was feeling alone and ignored by me.

Thank God, though, that by the end of that year we were back on the path together, and I know the Lord was pleased. I had learned to listen to God and was in a better place to lead my family.

Gideon, too, had learned to trust God's orders, and as a result, he was trusted to lead the nation of Israel for many years.

You Must Be Willing to Risk It All

I'll say this for Gideon: It took him a while to overcome his doubts and fears to trust the Lord's instructions, but once he did, he put everything on the line. Going into battle against an enormous army with a band of three hundred men "armed" with lanterns and trumpets was certainly proof of that!

Having decided to obey God, Gideon threw himself into organizing the task:

> Then he divided the three hundred men into three compa-
> nies, and he put a trumpet into every man's hand, with empty
> pitchers, and torches inside the pitchers. And he said to

them, "Look at me and do likewise; watch, and when I come to the edge of the camp you shall do as I do: When I blow the trumpet, I and all who are with me, then you also blow the trumpets on every side of the whole camp, and say, 'The sword of the LORD and of Gideon!'"

—JUDGES 7:16–18

During my time in the Air Force, I was privileged to work in the Pentagon, the nerve center and command headquarters for our nation's military might. There, the finest strategic minds formulate intricate plans for our missions and logistics across the globe. The very survival of our country could be at stake in any one of these decisions.

And I will tell you, I doubt *any* of those generals in the Pentagon would have thought much of the chances for Gideon's three hundred men surviving—let alone winning—a battle with a foe that outnumbered them a thousand-to-one or more! Miracles just don't figure into military planning—not now, and usually not in ancient times, either. God was literally asking Gideon to risk it all.

Recently, the president of our association of churches, Steve Riggle, had this challenge for our pastors: "When was the last time you did anything that meant certain failure if God did not come through?"

He was not talking about doing brash, stupid things that tempt God's forbearance. But think about this: If you can do something in your own strength, using your own resources and a plan you figured out on your own, you are not exercising faith.

Following God often means risking it all. Nothing God asks us to do is without risk. You may face the loss of your reputation, finances, relationships with others, and the comfortable life as you know it. But the more you obey God, the more you trust Him, His grace becomes bigger than the risk you face!

REFLECTIONS

Everyone wrestles with insecurity.

- Have you ever shared with someone else about your struggles in this area?

- Do you have someone you can share with?

- Which of the six lessons from the life of Gideon touched areas where you struggle?

- Did God give you some direction as you read this chapter? What can you do right now to obey that direction?

Stop right now and pray this prayer:

Lord, I admit that I struggle with insecurity. Forgive me for being too proud to even talk about it. I realize that I cannot do what You have called me to do without Your grace. Grow me in my trust and faith in You. Thank You that my insecurity only reveals my need of Your salvation. I commit to following the orders You give me and obeying them with a sincere heart. I commit my life to Your care. In Jesus' name, Amen.

Chapter Eleven

HELPFUL PRINCIPLES FOR THE LEADER

A NUMBER OF YEARS ago, I spoke to employees of a small insurance company about the keys to being an effective leader. Focusing on things God had taught me over the years, I shared with them a summary of the tough experiences, mistakes, and successes that had come, what I had learned from observing other leaders, and contemplating and applying principles revealed in my regular readings of the Bible.

Naturally, I had wondered about what kind of reception these faith-based ideas would find in this secular audience, but I was pleasantly surprised by the extremely positive response my message received. God has blessed similar speaking engagements before groups as varied as politicians, military leaders at home and abroad, and other pastors.

Now I want to share the same principles of effective leadership with you, trusting that they will help you become the kind of leader and person God intended you to be.

TAKE RESPONSIBILITY FOR YOUR FAILURES

Simply put, you cannot hide sin from God, and trying to cover up your failures doesn't work much better with mere mortals, either. King Solomon certainly knew that when he shared this bit of wisdom thousands of years ago:

> He who covers up his sins will not prosper, but whoever confesses and forsakes them will have mercy.
>
> —PROVERBS 28:13

I enjoy watching professional football. I remember getting a good laugh once when the color commentator, referring to a live shot of a place kicker who had just missed a field goal, said this: "Do you see who the place kicker is standing next to? He is next to the punter. Do you know why? Because the punter will listen to all his excuses for missing the kick."

Better yet, the commentator himself had once been a place kicker. He regaled his TV audience with his personal reservoir of excuses for those games where he had missed splitting the goal posts with a field goal or point-after-touchdown kick. Maybe the teammate holding the ball had been off on the tilt; perhaps the snap from the center was late; or there was that sudden gust of wind . . .

Whatever the excuse, though, the place-kicker-turned-TV-commentator said he always tried to find an empathetic audience (in other words, one that may share his viewpoint and even be inclined to use the same excuses at times . . . like other place kickers).

Aren't a lot of us like that place kicker, anxious to shift blame or make excuses for our failures in conduct or performance? We nearly shudder at the thought of admitting a mistake or a moral stumble. It is painful to come up short of others' expectations, and particularly to not meet our own standards!

What should we do when we make a mistake? *Admit it—right away.* If you are wrong, if you blow it, own it. Take responsibility. Acknowledge that failure to your superiors, to your subordinates, to family or friends, to anyone who is involved.

Then ask for forgiveness when your actions or words hurt someone, and next, foster an attitude of taking responsibility with those under your care.

These may be revealing, even uncomfortable questions to ask yourself, but do so now: Could someone under your leadership make a mistake and still keep his or her position with you? What about admitting when you are wrong—is that a sign of weakness or a sign of strength?

I was once fired because a comment I had made was misinterpreted. I was a junior officer, and a senior officer asked me to brief people on a number of Air Force programs. I thought a briefing was not needed, so I explained to him that I had already provided a short, succinct notebook for each person to review and then sign, confirming they understood the programs.

The leader was adamant, though, insisting on the briefing. I tried again to dissuade the superior, but he dug in his heels: *Do the briefing,* he told me. I could see I was getting nowhere, so I reluctantly followed his orders, making the arrangements.

Apparently, my attempts to talk him out of the briefing, even though I followed his instructions, did not settle well with him. Later that afternoon, I went by this superior's office and saw a huge stack of work on the desk of the leader's secretary. She was a great worker and wonderful Christian woman, and I only meant to compliment her when I remarked, "I don't know how you do it."

Simply, I meant that I marveled at her hard work and efficiency. But the superior overheard the remark and misinterpreted it to mean that I wondered how she could stand working for him. He wasted no time calling my immediate supervisor after I left, and I soon was told I had been fired at the superior's insistence.

I told my supervisor of the misunderstanding and set off for the superior's office to explain. But as I walked into his office, the Holy Spirit convicted me. You see, while my comment *was* misinterpreted, my attitude had not been. I suddenly realized that any protestations of innocence, while perhaps technically true when narrowly applied to that particular comment, would in truth be deceitful.

I felt the Holy Spirit was telling me, "Son, yes, he misunderstood you. But how about the whiny comments you made to others about the briefing assignment you were given? You were disrespectful and deserve to be fired. When you explain about the words he misinterpreted, tell him about your other comments he did not hear. Take responsibility."

This realization deflated any self-righteous tone I had. Instead, I was scared to death. But I knew that if I did not obey the Lord's direction in this, the situation was sure to get only worse.

I walked into the superior's office and told him he had misunderstood my comment. But then I told him that I had, indeed, made other ill-advised remarks to others about the assignment he had given me. Then I braced myself. *Not only will I still be fired, but now I've really opened a can of worms,* I thought.

I was stunned, however, as I watched the leader's reaction. There were tears in his eyes. He told me that the words he had overheard and misinterpreted were very hurtful. He was glad to know that he had misinterpreted the statement and proud that I had been honest about the other comments. Not only was I no longer fired, but he welcomed me back to my duties!

My knees shook as I left his office. I learned a powerful lesson about taking responsibility for my failures.

UNDERSTAND THE RELATIONSHIP BETWEEN PRESSURES, STRUGGLES, AND PERSONAL GROWTH

Having a bad day is not always a bad thing. That's right; sometimes, a bad day leads to good things, good outcomes! Mull over what the Apostle James had to say about this concept:

> My brethren, count it all joy when you fall into various trials, knowing that the testing of your faith produces patience. But let patience have its perfect work, that you may be perfect and complete, lacking nothing.
>
> —JAMES 1:2–4

You see, it is your struggles and those maddening pressures of life that end up being the very things that shape your character and walk with Christ.

My first Air Force assignment was to a large base in Georgia. I was newly married, and I felt very insecure about my first job in the service. I was thousands of miles away from friends and family, and those southerners' accents confused my native Montanan ears. My civilian government employees were not overly impressed by, or thrilled with, working for young, wet-behind-the-ears military officers.

In fact, one of those civilian workers bluntly put me on notice: "I cannot stand young military leaders in general, but I will let you know later what I think about you." Oh, yes, I felt about as welcome as Union General Sherman must have as he and his Yankee army pillaged Georgia during the Civil War!

You will not be surprised to hear that this assignment was very difficult for me, at least at first. My inner strength was challenged at a level it had never been before, as was my confidence. The demands of the job aroused insecurities I had no idea were lurking within me.

But after four years, I not only left Georgia a changed person, but I also left with an office full of friends. I was stronger from being stretched on the inside, and I was grateful to God for my inner growth. He knew the perfect situation to bring me into a new level of maturity, both as a leader and a believer.

Success and personal growth come through being faithful in difficult circumstances. As we work hard, run toward our problems, and ask God to grow us in character, He shapes us into a man or woman He can use.

Here is what God has taught me about pressures and struggles we face:

- Your trials will make you better or bitter; the choice is yours.

- Your attitude, not your abilities, is the key to your growth and destiny. Attitude is a choice.

- Every worthwhile thing has a price.

- Don't always try to step in and relieve the pressure from your children and subordinates. Maybe God is using the pressure to grow them; perhaps they just need encouragement to keep going.

MAINTAIN A SENSE OF PERSPECTIVE ABOUT WHAT IS AND IS NOT IMPORTANT

The Bible recounts an occasion when some religious leaders were testing Jesus, asking Him which commandment was the most important. Here is what transpired:

> But when the Pharisees heard that He had silenced the Sadducees, they gathered together. Then one of them, a lawyer, asked Him a question, testing Him, and saying, "Teacher, which is the great commandment in the law?"
>
> Jesus said to him, "You shall love the Lord your God with all your heart, with all your soul, and with all your mind. This is the first and great commandment. And the second is like it: You shall love your neighbor as yourself. On these two commandments hang all the Law and the Prophets."
>
> —MATTHEW 22:34–40

The answer Jesus gave these religious interrogators was succinct, short, and profound. The Lord provided us with a framework for how to live a godly life and how to put our focus and energy into what is truly important.

First, we are to give our lives to Him, wholly and without reservation. He is the filter through which we view life for all the decisions we need to make.

Second, we are to love and put others ahead of ourselves. If something or someone shifts our eyes off of loving and serving God and others, we get into trouble. If we start thinking and acting like we are the center of the universe, we have missed the mark and need to reestablish our priorities!

I speak from experience—from my own mistakes and observation of others' gaffes—when I suggest that when we goof up, it is because we have usually fallen into one of two traps. The first one is treating everything as equally important; the second is sprung when we have trouble establishing priorities, and thus appear to have none.

When I was a young father with small children, I had questions about how to properly address the myriad of safety issues that face parents. I got some advice from a friend that really has implications beyond child-rearing and extends into leadership principles.

I was told that I needed to distinguish between "swing" and "flame" issues with my children. A "flame" issue, I was told, is one that has a potentially devastating and long-term impact on your child. For example, you never want to have your children learn the danger of a gas burner by allowing them to put their little hands over the flame! No, a good parent does everything he or she can do to stop that experiment from happening.

Then, there is the "swing" issue. When your boy or girl is first learning how to use a swing at the playground, there comes a time when you need to let them experience the thrill—and wise limits—of the swing on their own. They may slip out of the seat and get a scrape or sprain an ankle dismounting too high in the air, but the consequences are not as serious and sure as a second- or third-degree burn from a red-hot stove.

Life is full of swing and flame issues. The flame issues are ones that can either launch you into orbit or derail the course of your life. Swing issues are important but not as life-changing.

So, which issue is which? The Bible gives us some guidance on how to determine whether it is a flame or swing challenge that is facing you:

> But when the Pharisees heard that He had silenced the Sadducees with His reply, they met together to question Him again. One of them, an expert in religious law, tried to trap Him with this question: "Teacher, which is the most important commandment in the law of Moses?"
>
> Jesus replied, "'You must love the Lord your God with all your heart, all your soul, and all your mind.' This is the first and greatest commandment. The second is equally important: 'Love your neighbor as yourself.' The entire law and all the demands of the prophets are based on these two commandments."
>
> —MATTHEW 22:34–40, NLT

Did you ever take a moment to jot down a list of all the areas of your life? Do so now: family, work, ministry, devotional life, recreation, finances, etc.—all those areas that are important to you. Now, look at each of these areas and evaluate which of them are not receiving the proper attention and which are eating up a disproportionate amount of your attention and time.

This may prove disconcerting; it will certainly be revelatory. But such reflection is a very healthy thing to do. You may find that a small area in your finances, devotional life, or family is having a huge negative impact on your life and priorities need to be adjusted.

Let's do that! Sit down, pray, think, and write out some of the priorities in your life that are currently being neglected. Next, let those trusted others in your life in on the secret so they can help you make needed changes. Your spouse, obviously, should be the first in line.

Your foundation set, next pursue and enforce those previously neglected priorities. I am convinced that you will find, as I have, that a short time of reflection, evaluation, discussion, and course correction can pay lifelong, even eternal, benefits!

When I sense that my life is getting out of sync, I often find it is because I have let my focus on my life's priorities slip. It happens to us all. But there is good news! God helps us to discern between those flame and swing issues and to start viewing life through the prism Christ laid out in the passage from Matthew cited earlier in this chapter.

Stand Up for What You Believe

When I became a Christian during my freshman year at the Air Force Academy, I frequently found my zeal to be a good witness frustrated by pressure from unsaved friends to return to the old behaviors and attitudes. Instead of influencing and modeling Christ to them, I let them influence me negatively. In fact, I mostly kept my fledgling commitment to Jesus a secret.

Later I determined that I would no longer hide my faith. As I lay in bed one night mulling this over, the Lord deeply impressed me to kneel beside my bed and rededicate my life to Him. I also sensed that I needed to pray for my roommate who had no faith experience.

I decided to wait until my roommate had gone to sleep before praying. After about an hour had passed, I finally slid to my knees beside my bed. I prayed quietly and then slipped back under the covers, only to learn I had not waited long enough to avoid my roommate's detection.

With sarcasm dripping from his voice, he asked, "Did you just pray for me?" I suspect that God kept him awake to teach me a lesson about not being ashamed of my faith. As it turned out, his attitude changed as we then talked. He allowed me to share my relationship with Christ, and my roommate turned out to be very open to my testimony.

Jesus was very clear about standing up for what we believe:

> When He had called the people to Himself, with His disciples also, He said to them, "Whoever desires to come after Me, let him deny himself, and take up his cross, and follow Me. For whoever desires to save his life will lose it, but whoever loses his life for My sake and the gospel's will save it. For what will it profit a man if he gains the whole world, and loses his own soul? Or what will a man give in exchange for his soul? For whoever is ashamed of Me and My words in this adulterous and sinful generation, of him the Son of Man also will be ashamed when He comes in the glory of His Father with the holy angels."
>
> —Mark 8:34–38

Pretty clear, isn't it? Jesus placed great importance on standing up for our faith, and yet many of us still succumb (like I did as a cadet) to the fear of rejection. What we seem not to understand is that generally the world respects and listens to men and women who stand up for and live out their beliefs. Integrity may be a rare trait these days, but it shines out all the more to a sick civilization yearning for it.

Since that painful lesson of my youth about openly exercising my faith, I've learned to speak up early in new jobs and relationships, to let my witness become a natural part of my life, to let my faith be as much a part of what people know about me as any other characteristic they may note. In fact, I hope they will come to know me well enough that how I conduct myself in situations pleasant and unpleasant will remind them that I try to live by and react with Christian principles.

ALLOW FOR DIFFERENCES IN OTHERS

Whether in ways obvious at first glance or in ways more subtle and deep, we are all different from each other. I talked about this area earlier, but it bears another look. In fact, I marvel at how often God seems to put opposites together in business and personal relationships alike. We actually seem to be drawn to the strengths in others, as if we know instinctively that they shore up our weaknesses.

Many times God has given me a deputy who balanced my capabilities and temperament, or He put me under a leader whose strengths were the exact opposite of my own. As I learned to accept and embrace these differences, I found that the organizations I led or served in only benefited from the varying gifts displayed and functioned best as different personalities balanced each other for the good of the whole.

There are some commonly accepted temperament types. Do you know people who fit into any of them (perhaps yourself)? For example, Dr. Tim LaHaye has written a number of books about four temperament types: *melancholy, sanguine, phlegmatic,* and *choleric.* Or, you may have heard of the Jung-Myers-Briggs personality assessment model (it supports up to sixteen psychological types). There are many other tools to help explore temperament types that may be helpful, too, but the most important thing is to understand, allow for, and learn to enjoy the differences in others.

Dr. John Trent, the award-winning author of numerous marriage and family books, created the so-called *LOGB* (lion, otter, golden retriever, and beaver) framework for classifying personalities. For example, some people are like the American beaver—deep-feeling perfectionists, very hard-working, and uncomfortable around a lot of people. Others may be otter-like, seemingly carefree, friendly, and outgoing with everyone but lax on schedules, tending to making lots of promises and not always following through.

Then there are the folks whose temperaments are more reminiscent of the African lion—hard-driving decision-makers and take-charge people who are seemingly insensitive and more focused on the task at hand than people or their feelings. Finally, there are the people who seem to have the makeup of the golden retriever. The demeanor of such individuals is easygoing; they seldom seem to get upset, are peacemakers, and have a dry sense of humor.

Can you imagine a room full of beavers, sea otters, lions, and golden retrievers? It could become an arena for conflict, the beaver telling the otter to grow up; the otter telling the beaver to lighten up; the golden retriever telling the lion to calm down; the lion trying to eat the golden retriever; and so on!

Well, substitute everyday human beings for that menagerie of fur, flippers, claws, and snouts, and such social mayhem happens all the time in our families, churches, places of business, classrooms, and on and on. That's the risk. None of us are alike, and it would be a pretty dull world if we all were just copies of each other.

The Bible is very clear that God is the purposeful creator of our differences:

> Our bodies have many parts, but the many parts make up only one body when they are all put together. So it is with the "body" of Christ. Each of us is a part of the one body of Christ. Some of us are Jews, some are Gentiles, some are slaves, and some are free. But the Holy Spirit has fitted us all together into one body. We have been baptized into Christ's body by the one Spirit, and have all been given that same Holy Spirit.
> —1 CORINTHIANS 12:12–13, TLB

Now here is what I am trying to say: All of you together are
the one body of Christ, and each one of you is a separate and
necessary part of it.

—1 Corinthians 12:27, tlb

God help us if we fall into the trap of preferring people who think
and act like us or trying to force others to fit into our mold. God created us to understand and enjoy the differences in others.

Recognize a Person's Weaknesses May Be Overextensions of Their Strengths

Here's a powerful concept: If you want to know what a person's weaknesses are, push his or her strengths to the extreme. In other words,
our strengths can become our weaknesses when they are not sub-
mitted to God's guidance and control.

Think about it. How many people known for their steady and
unshakable personality seem to go out of their way to avoid change?
I've known some people like that, and I'm sure you have, too. These
"solid rock" types often steer clear of change because they cherish
things that are predictable.

Another example is the person who is very organized, logical, and
likes to gather all the information possible before making a decision.
Those seem to be wise qualities, but they also are traits that can land
you in a mental rut, afraid to make a needed, snap decision due to
perceived incomplete information. Sometimes leadership must act in
the moment.

Or take the very innovative person, that go-getter with all the
exciting, new ideas. Often along with that vision can come trouble
completing a job; they frequently struggle to put their great ideas into
action.

How are these observations beneficial to you? Very simply, if you
take your strengths to their extremes, you will understand the areas
where you will struggle when pushed to and beyond your limits.
Having realized that, you are better able to grasp the root of the weakness, and that begins the journey to making it a strength.

By nature, I am very steady and usually unshakable, but I have
noticed that these characteristics can lead me to be occasionally rigid

and resistant to change. This has been a struggle for me over the years, but I have made progress in becoming more and more comfortable with handling and leading others into needed change.

COMMUNICATE, COMMUNICATE, COMMUNICATE

James, in a masterful example of tongue-in-cheek wisdom, put it this way: "We all stumble in many ways. If anyone is never at fault in what he says, he is a perfect man, able to keep his whole body in check" (James 3:2, NIV).

I believe I know very well what James was driving at in that passage. When I was in a very key contracting position, I had the privilege of working under the tutelage of an incredible leader. This leader was one of the most innovative and engaging persons I have ever seen.

That said, his motto was, on the surface at least, amazingly simple: "Communicate, communicate, communicate." He worked very hard at keeping the information flowing up and down the organizational ladder. I learned that saying that motto may be easy, but it takes determination and consistency to implement it. Doing so, however, can make all the difference.

Experience gained as a military officer and from observing other leaders has taught me many useful lessons. However, four examples stand out above the others.

First, just because you know something does not mean that others know it also. Work hard at sharing your insights, expectations, and vision. People do not understand something until it is communicated to them. Do not make people prisoners of your un-communicated expectations.

Second, using only one mode of communication guarantees that your message will not reach everyone. Use newsletters, e-mails, verbal presentations, visual aids, and anything else that will help you get the message out.

Third, sharing something one time does not mean you got the message out. It takes multiple and varied communications to make sure others get the message. Again, communicate, communicate, communicate!

Finally, if you think you are doing a good job of communicating, you are probably in trouble. Good communication takes a lot of hard work and usually has nothing to do with how good a communicator you may think you are. The reality is that people generally hear not what you intend, but what they interpret from their perspective. So, don't be surprised when your message gets distorted. Make sure you give people plenty of time and opportunities to ask questions.

Visibility can be just as important as words in communicating. Manage and lead by walking around your organization. Get out where the action is! Talk to people. Try to be as visible and approachable to your subordinates as you can be.

REFLECTIONS

Do you take responsibility or blame others? Own up to your words and actions.

Do you understand that your struggles are God's tool to shape your life? Embrace and understand how God uses them.

Do you know the difference between a "swing" and "flame" issue? Not everything carries the same weight of importance.

Do you stand up for what you believe? The longer you wait, the harder it will be.

Do you embrace differences in people? Differences in others are not threats; they are part of God's wonderful design.

Do you understand that your weaknesses are extensions of your strengths? Insight in this area will greatly help you understand yourself and others.

Do you "communicate, communicate, and communicate"? Effective communication is the glue that holds things together.

Chapter Twelve

THE CONTENTMENT OF THE LEADER

CONTENTMENT. NOW THERE is a word that evokes all sorts of images and assumptions. What do see in your mind's eye when you hear the word? Maybe you see yourself on a beach, a cold beverage nearby, an umbrella overhead, sails on the distant horizon, and crystal clear waves lazily lapping at your feet. Perhaps your picture of contentment is instead a quiet evening and a warm breeze caressing you through a window as you slowly rock a baby to sleep.

And what assumptions do you make about contentment? Do you equate it with bliss, some otherworldly state of perfect calm and peace, or maybe heaven itself?

None of those descriptions matched the life experiences of the Apostle Paul. The punctuation marks of his life in the service of Christ included shipwrecks, snakebites, beatings, stonings, fleeing for his life from mobs, sickness, imprisonment, and eventually being beheaded. Nope. No contentment there, right?

Well, *wrong*. Paul wrote about true contentment, and it had little to do with bliss or warm fuzzy moments. It had much more to do with unwavering trust and stubborn, consistent faithfulness!

> I am not saying this because I am in need, for I have learned to be content whatever the circumstances. I know what it is to be in need, and I know what it is to have plenty. I have learned the secret of being content in any and every situation, whether well fed or hungry, whether living in plenty or in want. I can do everything through him who gives me strength.
>
> —PHILIPPIANS 4:11–13, NIV

In my years of service in the Air Force and then in pastoral ministry, I have had numerous opportunities to learn about contentment from the perspective of Paul. Yes, *learn* is the operative word here; contentment is not a quality that comes naturally to us. It develops over time as we walk with God.

So, to the Christian leader, what is contentment? Paul's definition to the Philippians can be summed up this way: *Contentment means to be satisfied and at peace regardless of the circumstances.*

Unfortunately, for most of us, our level of contentment is directly influenced by our circumstances. Finding the godly perspective of contentment can be nothing less than a full-scale spiritual war we wage within our hearts and minds.

THE TWO BATTLEGROUNDS

We find ourselves fighting on the first battleground when we are not happy with the basics of life: sufficient food, clothing, and shelter. Paul wrote about this all-too-human character flaw in a letter to his Gospel protégé, Timothy:

> So if we have enough food and clothing, let us be content. But people who long to be rich fall into temptation and are trapped by many foolish and harmful desires that plunge them into ruin and destruction. For the love of money is the root of all kinds of evil. And some people, craving money, have wandered from the true faith and pierced themselves with many sorrows.
>
> —1 TIMOTHY 6:8–10, NLT

Funny how little human nature has changed in the nearly two thousand years since those words were first scrawled with quill and ink on parchment! That is because the enemy of our souls, Satan, has not changed in his mission to divert us from being satisfied with God's provision, and in our hearts, many of us struggle with our carnal nature and the selfishness, greed, and empty desires that flow from it.

We are constantly tempted to detour from the path, our focus shifting from spiritual growth and purpose in God to the shiny things and status offered by our materialistic world. It is a sad truth that many leaders, both in the ministry and in business, have been morally and spiritually shipwrecked by living beyond their means. They yearn for the "easy life" that wealth promises.

When your focus shifts in this way, compromises come. Desire a life of ease, and soon you may be crippled by a lack of motivation to work at all, along with not wanting to have to be accountable to anyone and increasingly determined to acquire anything you see. The saying "Money cannot buy happiness" has been around a very long time, but it seems to be a human genetic flaw to keep proving that truth through self-imposed suffering!

Now, don't shake your head at that. Haven't you ever fantasized about winning the lottery or inheriting a fortune from a lost uncle? *Of course you have.*

You will find yourself struggling on the second battleground when you are not content with the position where God has placed you. None other than John the Baptist, who was the God-ordained forerunner of Jesus, addressed that issue with some soldiers who found themselves convinced by John's call to repentance and yet wondered if their professions could ever fit into service to God:

> Then some of the soldiers asked him, "And what should we do?"
>
> He replied, "Don't extort money and don't accuse people falsely—be content with your pay."
>
> —Luke 3:14, NIV

Apparently, it wasn't the kind of job these new believers had that mattered most to the Lord. No, God wanted to see the fruits of repentance: integrity and godly character that began in remade hearts and flowed out in proper conduct and attitude!

So often, though, we aren't happy with our jobs, we don't think others view our vocations with respect, and we don't think we are paid enough. Simply put, we have a spirit of discontentment with our position in life.

Well, you would not be human if you have never wrestled with discontentment. I certainly have, and as I look back on those times, I can clearly see that attitude made me less effective as a leader in my workplace, my home, and my church. God taught me in those times, though, and now I want to share with you some keys to contentment He revealed to me through various passages of Scripture.

KEYS FROM THE BOOK OF PHILIPPIANS

As I opened this chapter, I quoted from Philippians 4:11–13. Return with me to that section of God's Word. The Apostle Paul is again our professor, and he has much to teach us about some of the spiritual weapons the Lord has given us to battle discontentment.

Contentment does not come easy.

In verse 11, Paul told us that he had to learn how to be content. Contentment is not our natural state! Our natural state is one of self-ishness. So, God provides the courses and classrooms, in the form of our life circumstances, for us to learn contentment. The Lord wants us to learn that our happiness does not depend on those circumstances and that focusing on them will have us living in the future, not seeing and learning what God has for us to learn right now.

Bottom line: We cannot lead effectively if we are plagued by a spirit of discontentment.

God wants to bring us to a point of being neutral on the inside.

In verse 12, Paul confides that in learning contentment, he also had to learn to be satisfied not only in times of plenty, but in times of want. That is the attitude God wants from us, too. We must be free of the slavery to circumstance in our faith and dependence upon Him. We need to specifically pray for a spirit of contentment in *all* circumstances.

Ask specifically for God's strength and power.

Verse 13 has Paul assuring us that just as he discovered, we can do all things through God's supernatural strength, including winning the battle with discontentment. Remaining ensnared and crippled by discontentment is a sure sign that we are living by our own strength and that we are focusing first upon ourselves. So, ask God for His supernatural power in order to win this battle, too.

KEYS FROM THE BOOK OF 1 TIMOTHY

Let's return now to some scripture I cited earlier from 1 Timothy 6:8–10, and while we're at it, add the preceding two verses (vv. 6–7) for the sake of context:

> But godliness with contentment is great gain. For we brought nothing into the world, and we can take nothing out of it. But if we have food and clothing, we will be content with that. People who want to get rich fall into temptation and a trap and into many foolish and harmful desires that plunge men into ruin and destruction. For the love of money is a root of all kinds of evil. Some people, eager for money, have wandered from the faith and pierced themselves with many griefs.
>
> —1 TIMOTHY 6:6–10, NIV

Contentment will come only as we learn to focus on God and not ourselves.

This is another principle I learned the hard way during another time of doubt and challenge. Over and over, I would tell God in prayer that I wanted to please Him more than I wanted to please myself. I asked Him to convict and spiritually call me on the carpet when my focus drifted from pleasing Him to indulging myself. Such grand prayers we probably have all said at one time or another, and I found progress in this area to be grindingly slow.

The Christian musical group Casting Crowns sums up this common situation pitting spirit against flesh very well in their song, "The Altar and the Door." Consider this refrain:

> Oh Lord, I try
> But this time, Jesus, how can I be sure
> I will not lose my follow-through
> Between the altar and the door?

I found the answer to that question to be persistence. Keep asking, keep trying, and keep believing. I did that, and slowly I started to see changes in my attitude and heart. God is faithful to answer prayers that come from a sincere heart!

God will honor a righteous focus with abundance.

As the Holy Spirit patiently partnered with me to make needed changes in my heart, I was led into a more God-pleasing focus in my life. His emotional, spiritual, and, yes, material provision increased along with that clearer, correct vision. It was as if He could now trust me with more. He also gave me more responsibility as a leader.

It was amazing. By focusing on pleasing Him, God gave me the very things that I had been previously seeking. As Paul wrote in the passage above (1 Timothy 6:6), "But godliness with contentment is great gain."

We must give up our "right" to own things.

In verse 7, Paul reminds us of that final, inescapable truth of existence that we brought nothing into this world, and we will take nothing out. So, we are not to act like owners of anything. God is the owner, and we are His stewards. Everything good in my life is a gift from God. He can give it to me, and if He chooses, He can take it away. It all belongs to Him—provisions, possessions, and positions.

If we are not thankful with what we have now, we will not be content if we are trusted with more.

We all think that if we just had more, we would be content. That materialistic mantra has come to drive so much of the American, indeed Western, mind-set. (Just watch a few minutes of television advertisements and you will see constant appeals to self-indulgence, greed, and the myth of gaining status through things.) *But it is all a lie.* The message of 1 Timothy 6:8–10 in a nutshell? God wants to change us from the inside out, not from the outside in.

If our contentment is based on what we think will make us happy, we will never be happy. Circumstances constantly change, and as our lifescapes change, so do our desires. John D. Rockefeller, the early twentieth-century oil tycoon thought the richest man of his time, was once asked by a reporter, "How much money is enough?"

His answer may not have been exactly enshrined in the American Dream, but it certainly has been spray-painted like graffiti on the wall of our society's soul. "Just a little bit more," is what Rockefeller said. In other words, the hunger for wealth and power could never be satisfied.

KEYS BASED ON EPHESIANS

In the first verses of chapters 3 and 4 of Ephesians, Paul tells us something that seems, on the surface, to be contrary to his usual message of freedom in Christ. Actually, it is the foundation of that freedom. The apostle writes that he is "the prisoner of Christ Jesus" and "a prisoner for the Lord." Some amazing keys can be learned from these phrases of Paul's.

See God as the one controlling your circumstances.

It is not Satan and it is not you who control things in your life as a believer. God is in control if we welcome Him into the driver's seat of our lives. Paul had made this transaction with God; therefore, he was able to proclaim that he was "a prisoner for the Lord." If Jesus Christ is truly our Savior and Lord, then He is the Lord of our circumstances! Do you continually acknowledge His ownership and rule in your life?

Realize that God can use you regardless of your circumstances.

Paul wrote the epistles of Ephesians and Philippians (as well as Colossians) from physical imprisonment that eventually ended with him being beheaded for his faith. Yet these letters contain some of Paul's most powerful thoughts—birthed in adversity but anointed with great power.

In prison, Paul witnessed to some of the most powerful rulers in the world, including Nero, the insane, megalomaniacal emperor of Rome. This apostle was an extreme but memorable example that our circumstances are not limitations to God; they are only limitations to us when we allow them to be so.

REFLECTIONS

Have you been wrestling with a spirit of discontentment over your position or possessions?

- Ask God's forgiveness.

- Thank Him for where you are right now.

- Ask Him to help you to focus on pleasing Him, not yourself or others.

- Thank Him for His power to win this battle.

- Give up the right to own anything.

- Rededicate your life to the Lord Jesus Christ.

- Ask God to grow your character so He can trust you more as a leader.

Chapter Thirteen

THE LEADER GOD USES

I F THERE WAS a history written of the first statements spoken by humankind, a few seem obvious. "I'm hungry." "I'm thirsty." "Who am I?" "How did I get here?" But arguably close behind those inquiries would have to be this one: "Why him (or her)? What does he (or she) have that I don't have?"

It's the same when the question is about leadership. Have you ever thought about why God uses some leaders more than others? I know I have. I've wondered if it is just a matter of His unknowable preferences or if there are attributes that He has developed in those other leaders that make them more usable.

As a pastor and military leader for many years, I have seen otherwise talented people end up causing serious problems in the very churches and secular organizations they should be blessing. But I have also seen less-skilled teams defeat teams with obviously superior talent.

Just because someone has a wonderful gift, that does not necessarily qualify them to sing, teach, speak, or lead. We must realize our abilities are gifts from God and that merely possessing them is not what qualifies us to be a person the Lord chooses to use. It is God who qualifies and God who blesses yielded, gifted servants with the desire and opportunities to develop latent talents—and it is our heavenly Father who chooses the arenas where we will serve Him!

Nonetheless, too often churches and other organizations use the following criteria to select their leaders:

- Talent: a person's apparent abilities, gifts, and skills.

- Appearance: a person's looks, height, and weight.

- Intellect and personality: a person's education, learning, cleverness, friendliness, humor, and magnetism.

- Wealth: the money a person may have earned or inherited and the possible donation they could make to us.

- Influence: the people a person knows and the influential positions he or she has held.

All those factors, in and of themselves, are legitimate. But if those are the only criteria we use to choose our leaders, we will choose foolishly. We need to understand that the above categories are only outward indicators of worthiness. They really do not tell us anything about the person's character.

The first two kings of Israel, Saul and David, are excellent examples of what happens when the so-called obvious leadership traits are allowed to rule leadership decisions (in the story of Saul) and when character and other godly criteria are not only included in the mix but made the prime considerations (as with David).

SAUL AND DAVID: A QUESTION OF MOTIVATION

It was not God's perfect plan for Israel to have a human king. He had wanted His chosen people to be a kingdom of priests under His divine kingship. He used prophets and judges to guide them after they arrived in the Promised Land—something Samuel tried to explain to them while warning the people about the inevitable hardships a human monarch would bring.

The Bible tells us what happened next:

> Nevertheless the people refused to obey the voice of Samuel; and they said, "No, but we will have a king over us, that we also may be like all the nations, and that our king may judge us and go out before us and fight our battles."
>
> And Samuel heard all the words of the people, and he repeated them in the hearing of the LORD. So the LORD said to Samuel, "Heed their voice, and make them a king."
>
> And Samuel said to the men of Israel, "Every man go to his city."
>
> —1 SAMUEL 8:19–22

There was a man of Benjamin whose name was Kish the son of Abiel, the son of Zeror, the son of Bechorath, the son of Aphiah, a Benjamite, a mighty man of power. And he had a choice and handsome son whose name was Saul. There was not a more handsome person than he among the children of Israel. From his shoulders upward he was taller than any of the people.

—1 SAMUEL 9:1–2

It didn't take long, though, for Saul to go astray. He became overly impressed with his status and began obeying God's directions selectively at first, then ignoring and finally disobeying them altogether.

Now the word of the LORD came to Samuel, saying, "I greatly regret that I have set up Saul as king, for he has turned back from following Me, and has not performed My commandments." And it grieved Samuel, and he cried out to the LORD all night.

—1 SAMUEL 15:10–11

Samuel's entreaties notwithstanding, the Lord had decreed an end to Saul's reign. The prophet, who genuinely loved Saul, steeled himself to deliver the news to the man he had once anointed. The latest sin had been the proverbial straw that broke the camel's back: Saul had not obeyed the Lord's command to completely destroy an enemy and everything that enemy possessed.

Then Samuel said to Saul, "Be quiet! And I will tell you what the LORD said to me last night."

And he said to him, "Speak on."

So Samuel said, "When you were little in your own eyes, were you not head of the tribes of Israel? And did not the LORD anoint you king over Israel? Now the LORD sent you on a mission, and said, 'Go, and utterly destroy the sinners, the Amalekites, and fight against them until they are consumed.' Why then did you not obey the voice of the LORD? Why did you swoop down on the spoil, and do evil in the sight of the LORD?"

—VERSES 16–19

Saul tried to argue the point with Samuel, essentially saying that he had, after all, *mostly* destroyed the enemy and his holdings. That didn't change the truth of his disobedience, however, or its consequences.

> And Saul said to Samuel, "But I have obeyed the voice of the Lord, and gone on the mission on which the Lord sent me, and brought back Agag king of Amalek; I have utterly destroyed the Amalekites. But the people took of the plunder, sheep and oxen, the best of the things which should have been utterly destroyed, to sacrifice to the Lord your God in Gilgal."
>
> —VERSES 20–21

Finally, Saul acknowledged his sin. But still, he had an excuse. His repentance was, like his obedience to God, only partial.

> Then Saul said to Samuel, "I have sinned, for I have transgressed the commandment of the Lord and your words, because I feared the people and obeyed their voice."
>
> —VERSE 24

Saul's appeal was rejected; the verdict was in. Saul finally realized the future was dark for him, but he thought he could still salvage appearances, at least for the time being.

> So Samuel said to him, "The Lord has torn the kingdom of Israel from you today, and has given it to a neighbor of yours, who is better than you. And also the Strength of Israel will not lie nor relent. For He is not a man, that He should relent." Then he said, "I have sinned; yet honor me now, please, before the elders of my people and before Israel, and return with me, that I may worship the Lord your God." So Samuel turned back after Saul, and Saul worshiped the Lord.
>
> —VERSES 28–31

Samuel and Saul parted, but the ordeal still weighed heavily on the prophet's heart and spirit. The Lord didn't let His servant sulk, however. Samuel had work to do, and God had chosen a new leader for His people:

> Now the LORD said to Samuel, "How long will you mourn
> for Saul, seeing I have rejected him from reigning over Israel?
> Fill your horn with oil, and go; I am sending you to Jesse the
> Bethlehemite. For I have provided Myself a king among his
> sons."
>
> —1 SAMUEL 16:1

Samuel was back on course. But the prophet, despite his decades in
God's service, still had much to learn—and the Lord was, as always, in
the mood to teach:

> So Samuel did what the LORD said, and went to Bethlehem.
> And the elders of the town trembled at his coming, and said,
> "Do you come peaceably?"
>
> And he said, "Peaceably; I have come to sacrifice to the
> LORD. Sanctify yourselves, and come with me to the sacrifice."
> Then he consecrated Jesse and his sons, and invited them to
> the sacrifice.
>
> So it was, when they came, that he looked at Eliab and said,
> "Surely the LORD's anointed is before Him!"
>
> But the LORD said to Samuel, "Do not look at his appear-
> ance or at his physical stature, because I have refused him. For
> the LORD does not see as man sees; for man looks at the out-
> ward appearance, but the LORD looks at the heart."
>
> —VERSES 4–7

Here is how the Lord proceeded to show Samuel just what He meant,
truly looking beyond the rugged field garb and sunburned brow of a
shepherd boy to see the heart of a leader:

> And Samuel said to Jesse, "Are all the young men here?" Then
> he said, "There remains yet the youngest, and there he is,
> keeping the sheep."
>
> And Samuel said to Jesse, "Send and bring him. For we will
> not sit down till he comes here." So he sent and brought him in.
> Now he was ruddy, with bright eyes, and good-looking. And
> the Lord said, "Arise, anoint him; for this is the one!" Then
> Samuel took the horn of oil and anointed him in the midst of

his brothers; and the Spirit of the Lord came upon David from
that day forward. So Samuel arose and went to Ramah.

—VERSES 11–13

SIX ATTRIBUTES THAT DISTINGUISH
THE LEADERS GOD USES

Consider these character traits and qualities common to the most
effective of the Lord's servants.

1. They have given their talents back to God.

Saul and David both brought talents to the throne of Israel, but
there was one huge difference between the men: their willingness to
surrender their "rights" over exercising those abilities to God. Saul
never gave his talents to God. He relied on his good looks, stature, and
wealth. What's more, he thought those things somehow continued to
qualify him to be the king.

David, on the other hand, was a man who gave back to God. There
is the irony about the gifts that God gives you: The Lord will not fully
use them until you give them back to Him!

Once this transaction is made, God pours His anointing oil on
those gifts and adds blessings and power to them and to you. The act
of giving back our talents to the Lord makes them instruments of His
ministry, tools with which the Holy Spirit can work such miracles as
encouragement, change, healing, and empowerment.

Are you holding on to gifts and talents that need to be given back to
God? If so, now is the time to give Him your talents and gifts! Open
the door to His blessings and see the power of the Holy Spirit flow
through your ministry. Tell God, "Lord they are gifts from You. They
don't qualify me or make me more special than anyone else. They are
only indicators of my calling. May I be called, chosen, and faithful
according to Matthew 22:14, which says, 'For many are called, but few
are chosen.'"

2. They are more interested in how God sees them than how other
people see them.

Saul's motivations and character are revealed by how he responded
to Samuel when confronted with his sin (see 1 Samuel 15:30). Saul
was more interested in looking good in front of his people than in

genuinely dealing with his sin. After being confronted, he gave lip service, essentially uttering the modern equivalent of, "Yeah, whatever. I sinned. Uh, Samuel? Let's keep this between us, OK? No reason for the people to know anything's wrong, right?"

When you sing, teach, speak, or stand in front of a group, what goes through your mind? Are your thoughts something like these: *Do I look good? Do they like me? Did I say it right? Did I present a good image?*

The truth is that we will never sing that song, speak about that topic, or clothe or groom ourselves to perfection. *We are human, and we will make mistakes.* In fact, when you think about it, isn't it amazing that God chooses to use us at all, given our selfish nature?

The right focus is to ask God to minister through us, to let people see Him and not us, and to please God regardless of what happens.

From my military days, I recall a story that made the rounds about an ambitious, self-serving Air Force wing commander. Everyone assumed this man was on the fast track to becoming a general. The time came when his wing was subject to inspection. When the inspection was complete, this commander asked the officer in charge of the team how he had done in this review.

The answer came in the form of his being immediately removed from command! The reason? The wing commander was deemed to be too interested in himself and not devoted enough to the overall performance of his organization. The lesson? Self-focus is a leadership killer!

3. They are willing to accept feedback from others.

Are you open to learn from others? Are you approachable? Or do you always have to be right? If you cannot or will not receive feedback from others, you are not a leader that God can trust in the long run.

Are you like the flawed King Saul, offering only excuses when confronted by your wrongdoing or failures of character? Or do you strive to be like King David, able to learn from your shortcomings and willing to seek forgiveness in order to serve God?

At a church, there was a woman attending who was a widowed pastor's wife. On a couple occasions, her actions had disrupted the worship services, so the pastor had to speak with her about it. He braced for an angry response—and got just the opposite. Indeed, her response, compared to how so many Christians today react to any criticism at all, was simply *incredible.* "Pastor, I will not do that anymore. I always want to be teachable and open to learn new things. Thank you for talking to me," she said.

As her future behavior showed, she truly meant every word she said. She stayed in the church, became very involved, and was loved by everyone. Because of her teachable attitude, despite her many years in ministry as a pastor's wife, she became a blessing to the church family, not the bitter, negative soul so many Christians can be when they are challenged about areas of their lives.

4. They are humble and repentant when confronted about sin.

As noted earlier, Saul really never did repent when confronted about his disobedience to God. Instead, he tried to justify himself to Samuel, shifting the blame onto his subjects. "Hey, the people made me do it! I tried, Samuel—I really did—to do what God wanted…but it was just too hard!"

Well, don't get too smug. A truthful comparison of our own actions today with those of Saul millennia ago shows how little the hearts of people have changed. Really, now. Doesn't Saul's squirming sound a lot like what you and I have done when faced with judgment? Don't we try to justify ourselves, telling anyone who will listen just how hard it was to do the right thing? Perhaps you recall a time or two when your excuse was that no one understood the situation you faced.

What happens when strategies to avoid blame fail? We often blame others. We become "spear throwers," just like King Saul did when he repeatedly tried to kill his eventual successor, David (see 1 Samuel 19 and 20). We are at fault, but instead of shouldering the blame, we attempt to eliminate those we see as a threat to our exposed weaknesses of character.

The key here to what God wants in His servants when they are confronted with sin: take responsibility and then trust the Lord to sort out all the nuances of blame. This can be as simple as it is difficult, but every leader should learn to use these heartfelt words: *I am sorry; I was wrong; and will you please forgive me?*

5. They are willing to do the right thing even when others won't.

Let's return for a moment to the account in 1 Samuel 15:24. Saul told Samuel that he had sinned because he feared the people and so he obeyed their voice instead of God's. This same aversion to riling up our constituents often rules the decisions leaders make today, too.

How many times do we do something because we don't want to offend others, even when following their wishes runs contrary to our own convictions? The truth is that it is very hard to stand alone. There will always be pressure to do things that please others, and few people want to stand alone against the mob.

But the real risk of such compromise is the longevity and effectiveness of your leadership. You won't last long as a leader if you are unable to find the courage to stand up to the crowd. The Bible is full of accounts where God called His leaders to stand tall, even when doing so meant being a solitary figure in a sea of angry opponents.

I remember a story that an English missionary told about a young girl in then-Communist Romania who stood up to her atheist teacher. The girl was a Christian, and every day she endured the taunts of this unbeliever until, one day, she could stand it no more.

The teacher told the class that Jesus was not real. If He were real, the skeptic insisted, everyone would be able to see and touch Him. The teacher then challenged those who believed Jesus was real to call out to Him. If Jesus was real, then surely He would come when they called!

There were a number of Christian students in the class, and they all hung their heads when the teacher made her challenge. But not the young girl. She mustered her courage and told the class, "Yes, we will call out to Jesus, and He will come. Let's call out right now." Her fellow believing classmates rallied and joined the girl in calling out to Jesus.

Here's the amazing part, and the missionary insisted it was true. Suddenly, the classroom doors opened and Jesus walked in! The teacher ran out proclaiming, "He came after all! He came after all!"

Standing alone is not easy, but Jesus responds to such courage.

6. They appreciate small things.

Sometimes we don't appreciate the seemingly little blessings we have, always yearning for what we see as the bigger and better things of life. God convicted me a number of years ago with this thought: "Every big thing that has happened in your life began as a small thing."

That certainly was the case for David. When Samuel first met him, David was not king. David was the runt of Jesse's sons, so low on the family totem pole that he was left with the sheep while the rest of the boys got to meet with the prophet. Even when this youth was reluctantly called in to stand before him, Samuel had no reason to look at him and see the man who would become the greatest of Israel's kings.

So, don't despise the seemingly small things God brings into your life as a leader, either! How we handle the little things determines whether God will trust us with bigger missions and callings He has before us.

We often want more resources even before we have begun to use what God has already given us. Little in God's hand is much. What are you doing with what God has given you now?

REFLECTIONS

God wants to use us all. The key ingredient is not the talent we have but whether we have given those talents back to Him.

Our character, not our abilities or talent, is what qualifies us to be used by God. He will reject the most talented person in the world who isn't interested in growing in character. Conversely, He will use less talented people who let Him grow their character.

- How well do you stack up in the attributes that were discussed in this chapter?

- Have you given your talents back to God?

- Are you more focused on what God thinks about you than what others think?

- Are you open to feedback and correction?

- Are you humble and repentant when confronted with sin?

- Are you willing to stand alone for what is right?

- Do you appreciate the small things?

Remember again these thoughts from Paul, penned under the inspiration of the Holy Spirit, about those that God uses:

> "Brothers, think of what you were when you were called. Not many of you were wise by human standards; not many were influential; not many were of noble birth. But God chose the foolish things of the world to shame the wise; God chose the weak things of the world to shame the strong.
>
> "He chose the lowly things of this world and the despised things — and the things that are not — to nullify the things that are, so that no one may boast before him. It is because of him that you are in Christ Jesus, who has become for us wisdom from God — that is, our righteousness, holiness and redemption. Therefore, as it is written: 'Let him who boasts boast in the Lord.'"
>
> —1 CORINTHIANS 1:26-31, NIV

I hope you have enjoyed and benefited from what this book has shared about the qualities, character, blessings, and expectations of God-blessed and God-directed leadership. If what I have learned from prayer, the Scriptures, and experience over the years results in anything, though, I hope it is this one powerful, life-changing truth:

The grace goes with the chair!

ABOUT THE AUTHOR

S TU IS THE Executive Administrator for Grace International Churches and Ministries, Inc., where he oversees all the day-to-day operations of Grace International, an international association of almost 2,500 churches in more than fifty countries. Prior to assuming his position with Grace International in January 2008, Stu was the District Superintendent for San Bernardino, Riverside, and San Diego Counties in Southern California and the Pastor of Sonrise Christian Center in Sun City, California. Prior to becoming the Pastor of Sonrise, Stu was the Equipping Pastor for one year at Trinity Lutheran Church in San Pedro, California. He was responsible for adult equipping, home groups, the prayer ministry team, and a major church renovation. He has forty years of Christian leadership experience, including teaching numerous adult Bible studies, leading a large college and career ministry, serving as a youth pastor, and speaking at retreats, seminars, and numerous churches.

Stu retired in 1999 from the Air Force as a Colonel after thirty years of commissioned service. In the Air Force, he led organizations from five to six thousand people and managed multi-million dollar budgets. He has extensive experience in budget development/execution, personnel development, administrative systems, strategic planning/execution, and writing/speaking. He has a Bachelors Degree in Engineering Management from the US Air Force Academy and a Masters Degree in Business Administration from the University of California at Los Angeles. He and his wife, Debbe, have been married for forty-three years. They have two grown children, Andy who is a teacher in Sacramento, California, and Lisa who is a medical doctor in Portland, Oregon, plus three delightful grandchildren.

CONTACT THE AUTHOR

stuj@grace.tv

www.gracegoeswiththechair.com